GW00871525

YOUR
PRECIOUS
LIFE

Disclaimer

This book is designed to increase knowledge, awareness and understanding of issues surrounding mental health. It is not intended to replace the advice that your own therapist can give you. If you are concerned by any of the issues raised in this book make sure you consult a qualified professional. Whilst every effort has been made to ensure the accuracy of the information and material contained in this book, nevertheless it is possible that errors or omissions may occur in the content. The author and publishers assume no responsibility for and give no guarantees or warranties concerning the accuracy, completeness or up-to-date nature of the information provided in this book. Names and identifying details of persons mentioned herein have been changed to protect the privacy of individuals.

YOUR
PRECIOUS
LIFE

HOW TO LIVE IT WELL

Shane Martin

ORPEN PRESS

Published by Orpen Press Ltd.

email: info@orpenpress.com
www.orpenpress.com

© Shane Martin, 2016
1 3 5 7 9 10 8 6 4 2

Paperback ISBN 978-1-78605-001-4
ePub ISBN 978-1-78605-002-1
Kindle ISBN 978-1-78605-003-8
PDF ISBN 978-1-78605-004-5

For more information about the author and his work, visit
www.moodwatchers.com
Twitter @moodwatchers
Facebook moodwatchers

A catalogue record for this book is available from the British
Library. All rights reserved. No part of this publication
may be reproduced, stored in a retrieval system or trans-
mitted in any form or by any means, electronic, mechan-
ical, photocopying, recording or otherwise, without the
prior, written permission of the publisher.

This book is sold subject to the condition that it shall not,
by way of trade or otherwise, be lent, resold, hired out, or
otherwise circulated without the publisher's prior consent
in any form of binding or cover other than that in which
it is published and without a similar condition including
this condition being imposed on the subsequent purchaser.

Typeset by Marsha Swan
Printed in Dublin by SPRINTprint Ltd.

contents

To Deirdre, Sorcha and Dáire

preface

One truth for each of us is that we only live this life once. It's a very precious life for that reason. Our journey on earth is an imperfect one. We will encounter challenges and crises. But I still believe that we are entitled to have the best possible life despite these setbacks. Unfortunately many of us are *sleepwalking*. We are like passengers on the train of life. Sometimes the train has to crash before we realise what is important about this life. People nearly have to lose treasures like health and happiness before they truly value them. This is because it's too easy to become lost in the noise of life: rushing, fussing, and stressing. The years pass by quite quickly. We need to wake up to our true potential to have as much happiness as humanly possible and enjoy the best of good health.

Over many decades science has made a wonderful contribution in understanding negative emotion. The emphasis on deficits, disorders and disease has allowed for effective interventions to be developed in order to support people who are unwell or unhappy. We will always need to reach out to these people with the highest levels of competency and, above all, compassion. However, while building a strong science and practice of treating mental illness, psychology had largely forgotten about everyday well-being. Through its obsession with illness, it can be charged with neglecting wellness. The best psychology tends to be kept in storage and offered to people who have taken a hit.

In recent decades psychology has experienced a welcome shift in its emphasis and approach. A growing number of psychologists have come to realise that research into what is wrong with people has potentially been conducted at the expense of understanding what is right in people too. What makes people flourish as contented and fulfilled human beings is as relevant as what makes people fail to reach their true potential. As well as designing interventions to help people recover, there is a need to devote the same resources to helping people become more resilient. We can sow the seeds of mental wellness as well as understand mental illness.

Why wait until we are unwell to learn about becoming healthier? Why wait until we are unhappy to explore what happiness means? If crises are inevitable, we should learn how to become more resilient in advance of these challenges. Psychology can offer pathways to help us stay strong as well as understand how we become weak. We can apply evidence-based scientifically validated strategies to experience greater fulfillment and become healthier.

As a psychologist I am passionate about empowering people with their true potential to bring about positive change in their lives. I have dedicated most of my professional life to teaching people the very best psychology to enhance the quality of their lives.

Too many people are wishing, hoping and praying for outcomes that they can influence greatly themselves. We continuously underestimate our potential to enhance the quality of our days and live more meaningful and fulfilling lives. In this book I share some of the best self-help tips from the latest scientific studies in the knowledge that everyone has a precious life to live – they only need to tap into their inner capacity to live it well.

Shane Martin, Reg. Psychol., Ps.S.I.
Sligo, August 2016

acknowledgments

To Hilda, whose idea it was for me to write this book
To Ailbhe, for offering me the opportunity to have it published
To Deirdre, without whose encouragement and support this book
would not have been completed
To Fiona and Marsha, for their editorial expertise
To Dáire, for his photography

1| in pursuit of a 'good' life

*'Not life, but good life,
is to be chiefly valued.'*
—Socrates

My heart skipped a beat when I opened the letter confirming that I had been offered the post of regional psychologist with the National Training and Development Institute. The progression from teacher to psychologist was now complete. I had taken a huge risk giving up a permanent, pensionable job as a secondary-school teacher. Studying for my master's in Applied Psychology at the University of Ulster in Jordanstown, Belfast, had been very stressful, particularly with the broken sleep that followed the birth of our first child, but I now had a job to justify all my efforts. I celebrated the good news with family and friends: I was now in a permanent and pensionable position again. I felt vindicated; my chosen path seemed to have been validated. What made it even more fortuitous was the fact that I didn't have to uproot my family, sell our home and start all over again in a different part of Ireland. When I look back on that celebratory meal, however, I realise just how naive I was at that time. There is a huge jump from textbook psychology to real-life psychology. My new job was going to make that abundantly clear.

Mixed with the excitement of settling into my new position was a deep anxiety. I would be serving centres in Monaghan, Cavan, Dundalk and Navan. Within these centres, programmes were offered to people who needed support to reconnect with their communities, acquire skills that would make them employable, overcome some traumatic event in their lives or negotiate their way through obstacles often associated with disability. Over the next number of years I was going to meet hundreds of broken people – people who had found themselves lost in the fog of life. I met many suffering from depression; people who had fallen into the darkness for so long that they questioned whether there was any such thing as light any more. My anxiety during the first few weeks of my job was heightened by recognising some of the faces. The fact that one of the centres was in the town I lived in brought the reality of mental illness home. Mental illness has a shattering effect on families. There is a thin line between wellness and illness and I was now meeting people who had crossed it.

Certain faces stay with me. I remember the friendly woman who used to work at the reception desk in a busy supermarket. I hadn't seen her in years; I had assumed that she had moved from the area. But she hadn't. I was now her psychologist. The student who had achieved wonderful results in her school exams and was the talk of the town but who didn't finish first year in her chosen university, I now knew why. And that nuisance of a man who was drunk most nights outside a particular pub in one of the towns that I regularly drove through. I'd considered him a scourge to his family and community. I now discovered that he suffered from addiction and had a shattered family who loved him dearly. Later I was to learn that he had made great efforts to kick his addiction over the years.

It dawned on me that I had an important job. Many people were attempting to make their own 'comeback' and were seeking guidance. Psychology was going to make me a more compassionate human being.

When I look back on my earlier years of being a psychologist, I realise what a privileged position I was in. Everyone has a story to tell. I became acutely aware of how vulnerable we human beings are. I listened to many stories. The people I met had three things in common. First was that they were very unwell. Many of them were in the depths of depression. Their lights had gone out. They were no longer working. Their zest for life had evaporated. The second characteristic they shared in common was that they used to be well. Each person could tell me about a time when things were fine, when there was a spring in their step, when they had a job that they loved, when they sucked in the oxygen of life. That time was in the past and they looked to me to bring them back there. The third point they had in common was that they took their health for granted. No one chooses illness from the menu of life. No one wants to be unwell. But there is a thin line. No one wants to stay depressed, either (despite some theories). Depression is a state of hopelessness that engulfs a person.

After about two years in any new position, most of us develop a sufficient level of competency that helps us become confident in our roles and responsibilities. That confidence allows us to appraise our efforts or to ask deeper questions about what we are doing. We may even question or positively challenge the system and propose new approaches or alternative objectives and goals. I didn't do that but I did begin to wonder privately about my work and its value. Meeting broken people is humbling. I certainly could not be found wanting in the efforts that I made to instil hope and point these vulnerable people towards greater health and fulfilment. But as I became more competent in my work, I began to arrive at two conclusions that were to change the course of my professional life, inevitably leading me to leave my wonderful job with the National Training and Development Institute.

I came to realise two things. First, many people in our communities become unwell unnecessarily and, second, many people stay unwell for too long. I was spending my working hours helping people to understand and alleviate their symptoms. This is crucial work and mental health professionals need to deliver such interventions with competency and, above all, compassion. We must always seek to help those who have fallen, but can psychology help in other ways? I found myself asking whether we were keeping the best psychology 'in storage' solely to explain to people what they should have done at a time of challenge and what happened because they didn't.

The Reality of Human Vulnerability

I have given many talks to community groups over the years. I remember being invited to visit a school on Árainn Mhór off the coast of Donegal. I had been asked to address teachers and a community group. I was trying to reduce the extent of my travelling at the time but an invitation somewhere like this intrigued me. I had never been on the island before. I brought my car on the ferry and received a warm welcome at the bed and breakfast. After settling into my room, I decided to put my coat on and go for a walk – to get a sense of the place and get something to eat.

The kind proprietor of the bed and breakfast informed me that none of the local pubs served food. What about the super-market for a sandwich? Closed. A Chinese or Indian takeaway? 'No such thing on the island,' she told me. I went for the walk anyway. It was dark and the winds blew aggressively. I could hear the sea gushing around me. I tightened my scarf as the coldness started to bite. I was surrounded by water and could see the lights of the mainland in the distance. This was a very different place to home or indeed anywhere I had ever been. I began to wonder whether I could give the same presentation to the islanders that I normally give to other community groups. Would it be relevant to them?

When I thought about it, I realised that I didn't need to amend my presentation at all. The reason being that no matter where I am or whose company I am in, there are three things that we all share in common. The first is that we are all vulner-able people. That was the same for the people on the island, on the mainland, on this continent and every continent. Everyone is an emotional being. We all know sadness, anxiety, worry and anger. We are not made of stone. Even the hardest shell can crack. Even the toughest can tumble.

The second factor in common is that we will all face chal-lenge and crisis as part of the journey of life. No one escapes. From the very beginning, things happen that we don't want to happen. Maybe the child who shares your seat at primary school breaks the beautiful purple pencil that your nana bought for you. Maybe, having spent hours designing a poster for the school art competition, it doesn't even win a place. Or your best friend dumps you. Or maybe later, at secondary school when romantic notions evolve, Mr Right turns out to be Mr Wrong, or indeed the other way around. Sometimes we work hard for exams with disappointing results. Or what we perceive as an excellent performance in a job interview does not deliver. Life is a wonderful journey but life experiences can hurt and wound us.

The third thing that we all share in common is probably the most important. We underestimate our potential to cope in challenging times. It is possible to keep hurt and health in the same room as each other. We do not have to fall apart in crisis. Many people stay standing during the storms of life. Lots of people thrive despite adversity. People who fall to pieces often learn to become stronger for the next challenge.

One major failing of our educational system is its failure to enlighten us about these three realities. It seems that we are practically obsessed with mental illness at the expense of understanding mental wellness. Why some people do *not* fall apart is something that science can investigate, as well as understanding why others do fall apart and designing interventions for such people. We can sow the seeds of mental wellness as well as responding to mental illness. We can explore the concept of happiness as well as determining what lies at the heart of unhappiness.

Three Wishes for this Life

When we think about the people closest to us, what would we wish for them in this life? If just two wishes could be granted in a contract – guaranteed to be delivered for the rest of your days – what would you want for them and indeed for yourself? It's a hypothetical question but it grounds us. What would you wish for? The answer comes easily to me – largely due to my work over the last sixteen years, in particular, and also from personal experience. When I think of the people closest to me I automatically think of my wife: I am blessed with a happy marriage. I also think of my two precious jewels – my daughter and son. I would wish for their health – that they would live long lives, that they would not be inflicted with complicated illness. Wouldn't it be amazing if such a wish could be granted? Some people have said to me that they would settle for that and that health is all we need. We know the saying – your health is your wealth. My father always said that once we had our health, we had everything.

But I offered two wishes. As you are allowed a second wish in this hypothetical exercise, what would it be?

This answer also comes quickly to me. Again, largely due to the work that I have been involved in, I would wish for happiness – that the people I love, and indeed myself, would be reasonably happy while we live on this earth. A long life with little or no happiness would exactly be that – a long life. But we have to be realistic about happiness. There will always be periods of unhappiness. The recent death of my loving mother was a period of immense unhappiness for me. What I mean, however, by happiness is that we would be happy more often than unhappy, and have a high average score for happiness for as long as we lived. Wouldn't it be amazing if health and happiness could be delivered in a contract – signed and sealed? What more would you want?

Sometimes people suggest a third element to happiness – money. Money does count. Research does show that if we do not have sufficient means to keep our home warm, to clothe our family, to put food on the table, that we will experience stress and find it difficult to be happy. During the recent recession, many people found themselves under severe financial pressure. This kind of stress can impact on our general health. We do need money. However, research also shows that accumulating millions does not enhance long-term happiness or affect our health in any positive way, other than allowing access to the best medical care. It seems that once we have enough, that is all we need. As a psychologist, I have met many rich people who do not know health or happiness. They have often wondered if they were ever happy. 'What is happiness?' they asked me.

It would be a wonderful gift to be guaranteed both happiness and reasonably good health for the duration of life's journey. However, I would probably seek a third wish. I think it would be wonderful to be blessed with a degree of resilience – the ability to stay standing during tough times. Life will always pose challenges, but with high levels of resilience we could probably protect our health more during those times. It would be great if we knew how to box cleverly during the inevitable crises of life, to know how to keep ourselves together, to be able to bounce back from setbacks and to adapt to the inevitable changes that are part of life's journey. As a former teacher, I see a huge disconnection between what happens in schools and what matters most in life. I have met many people with handsome results who are unhappy and unwell.

The remarkable fact is that although we all crave happiness, health and resilience, we tend to do very little about them. We tend to only talk about health and happiness when they have been lost. I have met hundreds of people who want their health and happiness back. Surely these concepts should receive greater attention, particularly within education? Of course, for a wide variety of reasons (to be discussed later), some people find it easier to be happier, healthier and more resilient than others. There may be genetic factors at play or the particular life circumstances of the individual. The specific nature of the challenges encountered may affect overall outcomes. However, surely if there is anything that we can do to make us more certain of being happier more often than being unhappy, or being mentally healthy and more resilient, we should be doing it. Surely, it would make sense to have a conversation about these vital areas *now*.

The Need for a New Psychology

When I first qualified as a psychologist, I was excited and couldn't wait to proclaim my qualification to the world around me. Maybe I was proud of myself. Maybe it was innocence. I had successfully changed career and survived a long, hard road of study and exams, coupled with work and family commitments. Soon, however, I discovered that it was prudent to be somewhat vague about my qualification. We talk about the stigma of mental illness but I think there is almost a stigma attached to psychology itself. As soon as anyone learned what I worked at (and in the beginning I was possibly too forthcoming), an uneasiness entered the conversation. Some people jokingly asked if I was reading their minds. Others asked if I found the work draining and whether I allowed all that depression to get to me. On discovering my qualification, some people withdrew from the conversation and seemed to become self-conscious of their every move and utterance.

For many people the word 'psychology' is associated with mental illness. This is despite the fact that there are many strands of psychology that do not focus on mental illness at all. I remember one funny experience in my hometown. I was walking up the main street when I was spotted by someone from my parents' generation. She left the shop in haste and called over to me; she was full of questions. How long was it since my mother died? Used she go to daily Mass? Where did my brother live now? Was the family home rented? Was I a doctor? Were there any Martins left in Carrickmacross? It was non-stop for about ten minutes. Then she started to talk about the recession and its impact on the town, pointing at shops that had closed. She suddenly paused. In deep thought, she scanned the street. Her head twisted and turned quickly as if she was checking for something.

Then she said, 'Would you mind coming into the shop to finish our conversation? It's just that people might be watching me talk to you for so long. They might think there's something wrong with me.' It's a funny story but does highlight the fact that psychology has parked itself so brilliantly within the domain of deficits, disadvantages and disorders that some people believe that it only has that remit. Indeed, when we hear that someone is attending a psychologist we assume that there is something wrong with him. We might even conclude that there always was.

I remember being asked to speak to a group of parents and the principal informed me that he hadn't told them I was a psychologist. He thought that it might have been harder to get a crowd out if they had known. Not for one moment am I suggesting that all psychologists are always perceived negatively, but I make the point that there can be stigma attached to the qualification.

Psychology has been a formal discipline for a little over a hundred years. Since World War II, it has focused most of its efforts on problems and potential remedies or solutions to these problems. It has made a wonderful contribution to helping us understand, treat and prevent what are termed psychological disorders. The classification manuals – *The Diagnostic and Statistical Manual of Mental Disorders* (DSM), sponsored by the American Psychiatric Association, and the International *Classification of Diseases* (ICD), sponsored by the World Health Organization, have allowed literally hundreds of disorders to be described, and facilitate a plethora of reliable assessment strategies and interventions to be devised for people carrying symptoms. The people who met me in the four centres where I worked at the beginning of my career wanted to know what was wrong with them, what caused it and how to put it right. There are many tools at the disposal of psychologists to provide such information.

But maybe, in its obsession with illness, psychology forgot about wellness. Why people don't fall down in crisis is surely as important as understanding and helping people who do. Understanding what the heart is of a sustainable happiness, inner peace and fulfilment in humans has to be as important as understanding unhappiness, frustration and anxiety. The reality, however, is that much of scientific psychology (until recent decades) has neglected the positive traits in human beings through its obsession in finding out what is wrong. Indeed, over 90 per cent of the books in the psychology section of any library are about what is wrong with human beings and how to put it right. The hard science has been reserved for the hard topics.

A watershed moment for the field of psychology arrived in 1998. Martin Seligman, a psychologist from the University of Pennsylvania, was president of the American Psychological

Association. In his presidential address that year, he urged psychology to 'turn towards understanding and building the human strengths to complement our emphasis on healing human damage'. That speech is considered to have been the launchpad for a new movement within psychology called positive psychology. This new movement was not an affront to traditional psychology. It was not an attempt to deny human weakness, vulnerability or flaws. It called, however, for a more balanced psychology. It asserted that what makes people flourish as contented and fulfilled human beings is as relevant as what makes people fail to reach their true potential. As well as designing interventions to help people recover, psychologists needed to devote their resources to helping people become more resilient.

As well as investigating weakness, psychology needs to explore scientifically the whole world of human strengths. I had believed that I was one of the only psychologists who thought like this. I was soon to discover that thousands of psychologists throughout the world had shifted the emphasis from illness to wellness and from unhappiness to happiness.

A Psychology of the 'Positive'

Positive psychology is the study of the conditions and processes that contribute to the flourishing or optimal functioning of people, groups and institutions. Seligman maintained that in relieving the states that make life miserable, it seemed that building the states that make life worth living was less of a priority. He and many other acclaimed pioneers of this movement were for the first time addressing the negative imbalance that had dominated the discipline from its beginnings. My excitement grew as I delved into the growing and propelling research being conducted into the 'positive' aspects of humans and their life outcomes.

At the beginning of my career, I met many people who were profoundly unhappy. Bringing them from minus five to minus two was progress. Psychology, however, can also bring people from plus two to plus five. We do not have to wait until we are unhappy to talk about happiness or wait until we are ill to talk about health. We have to make the best of the life we've got and, sadly, most of us have not acquired the education or skills to live what Socrates called the 'good life', or the best life possible. I have met hundreds of people who wanted a life worth living, people who wanted to know what happiness was and what was possible in terms of achieving greater happiness and inner peace at whatever stage of their lives they found themselves.

You can imagine how excited I was when I learned that eminent psychologists throughout the world were scientifically examining these areas. I could dip into scientific journals and follow groundbreaking new research, and propose strategies based on this material. Psychologists from the world of positive psychology were thankfully now addressing this 'bias'.

Living a Good Life

A life worth living is not merely an aspiration for people who are unhappy or mentally drained. Life is a relatively short journey and very precious. It doesn't matter whether you have a religious belief or not; one undeniable truth is that you only live this life once. We have no influence on when we enter this world and know little about when our natural death will occur. Everyone is entitled to the best possible life no matter what challenges or crises we encounter. Living a good life is what most of us really want, when we think about it, and has been the quest of some of the world's greatest thinkers. Philosophers Aristotle, Socrates and Epicurus each proposed his own theory on how *eudemonia*, their term for the 'good life', could be attained: through fulfilling one's capabilities, through virtue and knowledge, and through pleasure, respectively. Henry David Thoreau highlighted simple living and self-knowledge as the means by which inner peace in life is attained.

The people I met professionally wanted to feel good again. Many of them wanted to return to where they were before they became mentally unwell or distressed. But were they really as happy then as they thought? Were they living a good life or were they passengers on the journey? What *is* a good life? Today, the question remains as relevant as ever and psychology as a science has a unique contribution to make to this discussion. It has the potential to provide objective, verifiable answers to this most important question.

In order to understand what constitutes the good life and what makes this journey worth living, positive human experience must be understood. Positive psychology proposes that what constitutes a good life is a question about optimal mental health, happiness and meaning and from that perspective offers interventions to enhance it. But in order for psychology to make a meaningful contribution to this discussion it needs to have a firm grasp on mental health, not just mental illness. And in order to distinguish it from pop psychology, whatever theories emulate about living a good life, happiness or resilience must be grounded in a cumulative, empirical body of research. During the last number of decades a growing amount of research sought to understand the 'positive'. This research offers pathways to a better quality of life, to greater fulfilment and more sustainable happiness.

Becoming a Different Kind of Psychologist

I eventually gave up my permanent and pensionable job as a psychologist to pursue my passionate interest in the world of the 'positive'. Many people thought I was crazy. I did not leave because I was unhappy but rather because I wanted a new challenge. I wanted to be a psychologist who would empower everyone (not just those people who had symptoms) to a better quality of life. I was convinced that many of the people I met in the course of my earlier work should never have ended up speaking to someone like me in the first place. The best psychology does tend to be kept for people who have taken a hit. But psychology can also be utilised to prevent illness, to identify and harness strengths and to promote inner peace and greater life satisfaction. And, crucially, psychology can help people prepare for inevitable challenges and negotiate better outcomes. There was no job for this type of psychology, so I had to take a leap. It was nerve-wracking but I had to do it.

I designed a course called Moodwatchers, which would be open to the general public and focus on the science of health, happiness and resilience. The first course was delivered in the Iontas Theatre in Castleblayney, County Monaghan, about four-teen years ago. The plan was to offer a free talk to the general public – to educate them about what I was attempting to do with my new course. I wanted them to know what it was and what it wasn't before they enrolled. It wasn't a support group, although I have a lot of time for such groups. It wasn't therapy, although therapy works for many people. The course was a journey where, over a space of eight weeks, participants would learn and be encouraged to integrate strategies into their lives that were scientifically validated to improve their heath and happiness outcomes. I was nervous. I was attempting to de-stigmatise mental health vulnerability and demystify psychology. Would anyone turn up?

The course proved to be a great success and each week the class attendance grew. I knew then that I could travel with Moodwatchers. People seemed to want a course like it. They needed it. Over the following years, the course would be delivered at numerous venues the length and breadth of Ireland. Then I started delivering adapted versions of the content to management teams, teachers, students and parents throughout the country. As a former teacher, I knew how relevant the material was within the context of education. I ended up visiting literally hundreds of schools nationwide. More doors started to open for me. My work brought me into the studios of national television, radio and newspapers. It seemed to me that my pursuit of the positive was having a positive effect on my work and on myself.

It took time for me to feel secure as a self-employed psychologist and for people to become accustomed to what I was trying to do. But I have been blessed. Work led to more work and I became exceptionally busy. I have been invited as a key speaker to national conferences of the largest educational organisations in Ireland. I have lectured on the topics I am passionate about in universities and hospitals. I have worked with some of the most successful companies in Ireland within the public and private sector.

It all began with Moodwatchers – a simple, no-nonsense psychology course for everyone. I have received the most uplifting and inspiring letters and emails from hundreds of people who found it helpful. It seemed to arrive at the right time in their lives. It opened their eyes to their potential to become healthier and happier. It unearthed their inner capacity to turn things around for themselves. We are all so busy – rushing to the next thing or wondering about the last thing. But we often miss the bit in the middle – our life – our precious life. It's almost as if we are passengers on a train.

At the beginning of my career, I met people whose train had crashed. It's so easy to become lost in the noise of life, to lose sight of ourselves. We need to step back and learn about how to live life well. Through the chapters of this book I will share with you the best strategies I have gathered from what science has learned is associated with the best outcomes. It's never too late to be healthier and happier. It's never too late to embrace a better quality of life. This is called HOPE.

2| thinking straight

'*The mind is its own place, and in itself*
Can make a Heaven of Hell, a Hell of Heaven.'
—John Milton

I was due to meet Paula for the first time at three o'clock. There was a knock on the door five minutes before the planned counselling session. I greeted her warmly but she was stony cold in response. She uttered a 'hello' devoid of any real feeling.

She took her seat and sat upright in the soft chair. I asked if she'd like to take her coat off. She declined by shaking her head. I then asked some preliminary questions. Her face stretched with stress.

Paula was in crisis. Her husband had cheated on her after 25 years. The pace of conversation quickened as she became more emotional. Her tone became aggressive as she recounted her story.

I allowed her nearly ten minutes before I held my up hand and said, 'Paula, you mightn't be ready for someone like me just yet.' This stopped her in her tracks instantly.

'Why?' she said and she appeared startled, taking a defensive pose in response.

'Because you're too angry,' I replied. 'You have a right to your anger. What happened to you should never have happened. You are entitled to your anger and it needs a voice.'

My heart went out to her because of what she had experienced.

'But you're so angry now you can't hear me properly. You might be hoping that I'll agree with everything that you say and if I don't you might instantly decide that I'm a useless psychologist who you could never really talk to.'

The point I was making was that Paula was so emotionally distressed that she couldn't think straight. She could only hear herself. She was engulfed and governed by hurt and anger. She first needed to work on relaxation techniques to calm herself down. When she later tried meditation, she became calmer and was able to connect with me properly. When we are emotionally distressed we cannot think in a rational, logical or fair-minded way.

I remember attending the wake of a local farmer who had died. His wife was remarkably composed in the busy hallway as neighbours, friends and relatives streamed in to pay their respects. He had managed his small farm in partnership with his beloved wife for over 50 years. They were close companions and had made an excellent team. Over a cup of tea in the kitchen, I was shocked by something I overheard. Two women, friends of the widow, were conducting a conversation that seemed most inappropriate. Although her husband's death was expected after a period of long illness, their questions seemed completely insensitive to her situation.

'Will you be afraid on your own in the house? Who will help you with the farm? Would it be viable to pay someone to help you? Would you ever consider moving into town? Did you see the apartments for sale beside the church?'

Maybe, in their own unique way, they were trying to assure the grieving widow that she was not 'doomed' to live a lonely life and be afraid on her own. But a wake is not the best time for asking such questions of the bereaved. I felt embarrassed. But she answered them adroitly.

'I won't be making any decisions until four seasons pass. I'm too annoyed to think straight at the moment.'

And the widow was absolutely correct. Sometimes we cannot see through the fog of our emotions. Often the wrong decisions are made solely because they were made at the wrong time. Our emotions can distort our thinking but many of us are unaware of how our thoughts affect our feelings. We can engage in unhelpful, illogical and irrational thinking. We are more prone to this when emotionally distressed. We can quite easily lock ourselves into our own box with our own problems. When we are emotionally distressed, it is practically impossible to engage the voice of reason. I have often said that the greatest friend of depression is solitude. And you don't have to live on your own to experience solitude – you can detach yourself from the people you live with and become your own advisor, but you can sometimes be your own worst possible coach or enemy.

The transition from primacy school to secondary school is a major landmark in a child's educational career. Parents can feel deeply anxious about it. Breda was one such parent. She was very nervous about her daughter Sheila's transition to a large secondary school from a tiny rural school where her experience had been one of small classes and intimacy. How would

Sheila cope in such a huge educational institution with over 1200 students?

Breda became reassured on learning that her daughter would be in the same class as her best friend, Susan. Breda had been Susan's babysitter and both girls had practically lived in each other's houses for eight years. They were very close. Breda couldn't believe her luck when she read the list of names on Sheila's class list. Her prayers had been answered. Sheila would be okay once she had Susan with her.

But within a couple of weeks a crisis happened. A tearful Sheila rushed into the kitchen, threw her school bag against the wall and started to cry.

'What's wrong?' Breda asked in alarm.

'Susan has dumped me for someone else.'

'Are you sure?'

'Yes,' Sheila answered, 'she has a new friend now.'

Breda called her husband into the kitchen to tell him the news. 'Susan's dumped her! But it doesn't surprise me because her mother is a bitch too and we minded her children for free all those years. It's never too late to learn the calibre of your neighbours.'

This is an example of one emotional response being met with another. Breda drew conclusions without any rational exploration of the events of the school day. If she had asked some questions she might have discovered that her daughter had not been dumped at all. Susan just wanted another friend as well as Sheila.

Advice based on emotion is inevitably flawed. We often tell our friends or colleagues what we think they need to hear. It's not that we deliberately mislead but we sometimes do not stop and think. We rarely step back from such situations to hit the 'pause' button. When we are emotional, we are more likely to jump to conclusions, decide without evidence or build unfounded theories on our experiences. We need to learn to be more rational in our approach to ourselves, to others and to our world.

The difference between you and a piece of stone is the ability to think (with a few other differences, too). We are all thinking beings. The first thing we do when we wake up is have our first thought of the day. The last thing we do before we fall asleep is have our final thought of the day. Through brain-imaging technology, we have identified the part of our brain associated with thinking and this remains active even while we sleep. We are constantly thinking – constructing our own reality – remembering, anticipating, imagining. Most of our thoughts are never expressed openly. We think a great deal to ourselves. Often we conclude without evidence. I have met many people who have recovered completely from depression but no one who has succeeded without having first contemplated the thought that recovery was possible in the first place. Naturally, there is much more involved in recovering from depression than thinking it to be possible. But such thoughts definitely represent a good starting-point. Engaging in thoughts like this harness hope and allow for plans and strategies that can lead to such breakthroughs.

Addressing the Negative Bias
Scientists have often made the case that we humans are born with a negative bias. Often people ask me if this is an Irish thing: it's actually a human thing. As a species we have survived because of this bias. We sought out all other threats and eradicated them.

That's why we remain conquerors of the planet. From birth, we quickly learn how to defend, to anticipate threat, to have what others have, or to have even more. We learn to compete and win. We learn how to fight or take flight. It's as if we have been programmed. Children are rarely taught how to calm themselves down. Within our families or throughout the many years spent at school, most of us were never taught how to be rational thinkers. We never learn how our thoughts influence our moods. Or how sometimes we can think thoughts that make us feel worse than we should feel. Or how we can worry too much about things that are never going to happen. Or how we can get the wrong end of the stick. It is a pity that we are not taught from the early years how our thoughts influence our emotions. There are innovative initiatives taking place in some primary schools in Ireland but the true potential of teaching rational, objective and logical thinking has yet to be realised.

World-renowned American psychiatrist Aaron Beck has had a long and successful career. He is currently professor emeritus in the Department of Psychiatry at the University of Pennsylvania. In the 1960s as a researcher and scientist he designed and conducted experiments to test psychoanalytic concepts of depression. He was expecting his research to validate fundamental precepts of psychoanalysis such as the unconscious, repetition, transference, drive and so on. He observed during his analytical sessions that his patients had an 'internal dialogue' going on in their minds, almost as if they were talking to themselves. This private conversation was influencing their feelings and behaviour. Only a fraction of these kind of thoughts was reported by them to him.

For example, in a therapy session the patient might be thinking to him or herself: 'He [the therapist] hasn't said as many hopeful things to me today. I wonder if he's less hopeful about me recovering than he seemed to be last week?' These thoughts might make the patient feel slightly anxious or perhaps disappointed. The patient could then respond to this thought with further thoughts, such as, 'He probably realises that I'm a much worse case than he initially thought and that's why he's not encouraging me as much.' The second thought might significantly change how the patient is feeling but the reality is that the therapist might have as much hope or more in the patient's ability to recover but was, at that juncture, engaged in practical questioning of the patient's beliefs and thought patterns.

Beck highlighted the link between thoughts and feelings as he developed his theory. He invented the term 'automatic thoughts' to describe emotion-filled or 'hot' thoughts that might pop up in the mind. Beck maintained that people were not always fully aware of such thinking. Through careful questioning by the therapist, patients could learn to identify and report unhelpful, irrational and unfair thoughts. According to Beck, if a person was feeling upset in some way, he or she was potentially engaged in an internal conversation that coloured his or her mood at that time. Beck found that identifying these thoughts was fundamental to understanding and overcoming the patient's difficulties.

He termed these cognitions 'automatic negative thoughts' and their content tended to fall into three categories – negative thoughts about oneself, the world and the future. Patients rarely questioned how logical, fair or rational these very powerful thoughts were. As a consequence they accepted them as valid or absolute truths. Beck began to help patients think about how they were thinking. By helping them identify these automatic thoughts and evaluate them, they could determine whether they were helpful, fair or true. This approach helped them feel better emotionally and behave more functionally.

Beck's belief that how we humans think is linked to how we feel and consequently how we behave was at the time a revolutionary proposal. It pulled the rug out from under established psychoanalytic theories. Cognitive Behavioural Therapy evolved from this new theory. CBT, as it is probably best known, is the most researched and effective therapy worldwide for most mental health disorders.

CBT seeks to help people understand what is going on in their minds. It helps them step back, become aware of their automatic thoughts and test them out. It's not that negative thoughts should not be allowed. Sometimes negative thoughts are justified due to one's circumstances. But when we are in a state of distress, we may base our predictions and interpretations on a biased view of the situation, making the difficulty that we face seem much worse. Through CBT, people are helped to correct these misinterpretations.

Beck maintained that if his patients learned to become more rational and seek the evidence before they made any conclusions, they could prevent themselves from being trapped in depressed or anxious moods. By testing out rigidly held theories, patients could potentially free themselves from thinking mechanisms that impacted negatively on the quality of their lives.

Where Do Irrational Thoughts Come From?
But why are we vulnerable to irrational and illogical thoughts? Beck suggested that these thinking patterns are set up in

childhood, and become automatic and relatively fixed. A mother might praise her daughter during Granny's visit. The daughter may be asked to show Granny her dancing medals while her mother beams with pride. Then the mother asks her to show Granny her school report.

'Look at those excellent results. That's some girl we have here,' says the mother. 'Mary makes us very proud.'

There is nothing wrong in this situation. A naturally proud mother is affirming her daughter's talents to her granny, however, there may be another child observing this situation but engaged in a private conversation that affects them not just in that instance but as they continue to develop. That other child might be thinking, 'If only I won medals. It really matters when you win things. I wish I won prizes. I will never be Granny's favourite.'

Many people develop unhelpful belief systems not because they were directly taught them but because they learned them from their experiences through their childhood and teenage years. That observing child may learn that they must work hard to achieve affirmation and that affirmation is key. Such a rule for living (known as a 'dysfunctional assumption') may do well for the person most of the time and help them to work hard and achieve success.

However, if something happens that is beyond their control and they experience failure, the dysfunctional thought pattern may be triggered. As a consequence that person may begin to have 'automatic thoughts', such as, 'I am a failure. No one will value my input any more. I can't face the people I have disappointed.' This stream of thoughts will inevitably affect that person's mood and their approach to their life and work.

Beck described how our mind can convince us of something that is not true as a 'cognitive distortion'. These inaccurate thoughts are usually utilised to reinforce negative thinking or emotions. In truth, they only serve to keep us feeling bad about ourselves. For example, someone may be thinking, 'I always fail when I try anything new. When I think of it, I actually fail at everything I do.' This is extreme and rigid thinking. This person is seeing things in extremes: failure in the past means failure in the future. It's a form of learned helplessness.

This cognitive distortion needs to change or the individual will never realise their true potential. Their thinking will hold them back. They will first have to identify this unhelpful thought, explore its true validity by examining the evidence around it, and refute it. By refuting this negative thinking over and over again, it will slowly lose its power.

If Aaron Beck gave us the term 'cognitive distortion', the psychologist David Burns has developed it further and helped demystify it with commonly applied examples. You may identify certain cognitive distortions that you or people you know are vulnerable to from the list below. Later we will examine ways to potentially rid ourselves of such distortions.

Some Common Faulty Thinking Mechanisms

Filtering
This is when you select one aspect of a situation and magnify it. The magnification is always at the expense of even considering the positive aspects of the same situation. Mary invited all her neighbours and friends to her house-warming party. However, when she started to clear up afterwards, she discovered that the bases of her apple tarts were burnt. She started to torture herself

with thoughts about her friends having had to eat the burnt tarts. How embarrassing! How mortifying! She concluded that her party had been ruined. What must her guests think? She would never have a party again.

She failed to consider all the things that went right (these were all filtered out as she appraised the event). All the other food that was exquisitely prepared and enjoyed by her guests was forgotten. The music and sing-song were great. The atmosphere was happy. But the only thing Mary concentrated on was the burnt tarts.

Black-and-White Thinking

This is what I call 'two-card-trick' thinking. Either you are right or I am right. Either the event has been a success or a failure. Black-and-white thinking is a very rigid form of making sense of things. It does not allow for grey: maybe both of us are wrong – maybe both of us could have handled things better. Maybe the event had its successes and failures but overall was more than adequate.

Black-and-white thinking is usually at the heart of conflict. Your rights or our rights? Your flag or our flag? Your culture or our culture? The successful peace process in Northern Ireland brought politicians and communities into the 'grey' zone. Your culture and our culture. Your rights and our rights. Agreeing to disagree or meeting people halfway can form the solid foundations of a successful peace process.

John was always proud of his lifelong friend Raymond. They had been close friends through primary and secondary school. They had worked together on building sites in New York for decades. But Raymond learns that John has applied for a new job and hasn't told him. How could a genuine friend be so private, he wondered. Suddenly he wants nothing to do with him ever again. He is not a good friend any more. You are either a good friend or a bad friend, as far as John is concerned.

Now he concludes that Raymond is actually a bad friend. This absolute thinking does not allow for any 'middle ground'. It does not allow for the notion that good friends can sometimes let us down. As a consequence of this rigid thinking, John cuts his old friend out of his life.

Overgeneralisation

This is where we make a general conclusion based on a single incident or piece of evidence. When something goes wrong for you, the assumption is made that the same thing will always go wrong for you in the future. You convince yourself that it's typical of your experience of life. It is almost like a never-ending pattern of defeat.

Imelda does not get called for interview after applying for a job. She concludes that she will never be called for an interview. She never did so she never will. The reality is that many people are not called for interview but eventually do end up being employed. In fact, Imelda is a very young woman who has had little or no opportunity to apply for jobs and limited experience when it comes to interviews. Experiencing one or two disappointments does not mean that she will always be disappointed. That conclusion is far too general and deeply unhelpful.

Jumping to Conclusions

This is where you interpret a situation without rational analysis, where you decide something without truly knowing if it's a fact or not. While on your holidays you ran into a colleague, who seemed to move quickly away from you and was very evasive about her plans. It was almost as if she didn't want your company. You jump to the conclusion that she does not like you as a person. Indeed, you may decide to be less friendly to her in future. However, it may be that she had genuine reason to rush away. Maybe she was having an affair. Maybe her elderly mother was in another shop. Maybe she had her worries. You conclude without the evidence and as a consequence feel differently about your colleague. Such thinking may affect how you treat this person in the future.

Magnifying Negative Experiences

Padraig is very late for his lecture. He peers through the window in the door and waits for the lecturer to turn around to write on the board. He plans to slip in quietly when he does. His opportunity arrives. Padraig shoves the door open but somehow stumbles and falls through the door. His folders and pens scatter. Heads turn. His cheeks start to burn. He cannot find a seat and scans the rows. The lecturer stops speaking and points at a vacant seat in the front row. Padraig is truly mortified.

But instantly he starts to think thoughts like, 'I'm finished here, what does that lecturer think of me now? Everyone here must think I'm an idiot.' In his mind he decides that his reputation is damaged. The truth is that the lecturer doesn't even know his name and that everyone concentrated on the graphs on the board and took notes for the next 40 minutes. Nobody really noticed what happened. But even later that night Padraig is still talking about the fool he made of himself and how he will always stick out in the mind of the lecturer. Falling in the door was a negative and embarrassing situation, but Padraig is magnifying its importance. He is catostrophising. The truth is that most people aren't actually that interested in other people and simply don't notice them as much as we think.

Belittling Positive Experience

We can also belittle positive experience. Emer sits in the lecture hall and awaits the results of her recent assignment. The lecturer moves around the hall, handing back papers. Emer smiles as she notes 82 per cent on the cover as her paper is placed before her. She feels very satisfied and decides to text her mother about her excellent mark. Before she searches for her mobile phone she glances at the results of some of her peers. The student to her right achieved 90 per cent and the person to her left 86 per cent. She scans the row in front of her: 85 per cent, 88 per cent, 94 per cent and so on. It seems everyone has done well in the assignment.

She instantly concludes that the lecturer is obviously an easy marker. She even starts to check the work of her peers to see if those who did better than her wrote longer or more comprehensive answers. Some of them didn't. She is considering asking the lecturer for a meeting to determine where she lost her marks. All of a sudden, her excellent mark of 82 per cent counts for nothing. From elation to deflation within a space of ten minutes – all because of how she was thinking.

Personalisation

This cognitive distortion allows people to personalise negative experience and blame it entirely on themselves. This type of thinking ensures that a person translates what other people say or do as a personal reaction to them. They perceive themselves as the cause of the unpleasant event or experience. In the canteen, Julie reminisces about her school days and her friend

Maura starts to cry. Julie immediately assumes this is because of something that she said or did. She concludes that she has an uncanny way of upsetting people. However, Maura may have a reason totally unconnected to the conversation that preceded the upset. Sometimes such thinking is bordering on egocentric – where we interpret every reaction as personal.

Mind-Reading

Sometimes we decide that we know what someone really thinks about a person or event. We may even conclude that that person's views are opposite to what they have openly expressed. People applying this cognitive distortion tend to use phrases like, 'I know what she really means,' or, 'I can see it in his eyes.'

Jill has been asked to make a presentation to management about her vision for the future. She passionately lists out her innovative ideas about the company's change of direction. As she speaks, she keeps looking at the CEO. He seems stern-faced and appears unimpressed. Afterwards she tells her friends that she knew the CEO was unimpressed. She could see it in his face.

The following week the CEO calls her to his office to further explore her strategies for the future direction of the organisation. Whatever she saw in the CEO's face that day was obviously not disinterest or boredom. This became clear when he invited her to his office. He wanted to explore her 'wonderful' ideas. By 'mind-reading' she had made herself very upset all weekend. She even had a conversation with her husband about 'pulling back' at work because her input was never appreciated by management.

Fortune-Telling

This is when we proclaim to know what the future holds. It involves making negative predictions. Often these predictions of doom and gloom are vocalised and shared with others.

Jason is waiting anxiously outside the exam hall. He frantically rereads his notes for the final few minutes. One of his friends comes over to ask how well he has prepared. Jason replies, 'It won't make any difference. If you thought the previous exam was hard, this one will be worse. I'm going to fail anyway.' Not a very uplifting way to approach an exam, is it? What kind of emotions are being fuelled by such thinking? In this situation Jason is predicting the future and heightening his anxiety.

Curbing Irrational Thoughts
Can we fix cognitive distortions? It takes time and effort to unravel irrational thinking patterns. Some of the following strategies may help.

1. WRITING DOWN OUR THOUGHTS
Writing down our troublesome thoughts will put them in front of our eyes. I often use the analogy of the helicopter or aerial view. This is almost as if we look down on ourselves and try to see things from a distance. It is then that we can start to examine our thoughts properly. We could even determine whether they fit into any of the categories mentioned above. This kind of exercise helps us step back and promotes a rational approach. Over a series of days or weeks you may notice that the same cognitive distortion surfaces again and again. You may start to learn more about yourself during the process. You may also notice that as time passes you might feel differently about events because you are thinking differently about them. With passing time it is easier to be more objective and fair.

2. EXAMINING THE EVIDENCE

You may have to enlist the help of other people with this. You could ask them for their opinion of a situation and to propose alternative meanings. This will involve deliberately considering other explanations or theories and sustaining a conversation about them. You could start with the phrase 'Maybe I am making the wrong sense of this ...' Could there be other reasons or possibilities? This is sometimes referred to as 'surveying' – surveying other people's opinions. It is important to ask a number of people; seeking more opinions can help loosen the grip of distorted thinking. It's even more important to remind these people not to tell you what they think you want to hear.

3. APPLYING A COMPASSIONATE RESPONSE

This is where you consider the kindest possible explanation for what is troubling you. The conversation with yourself or a friend would be built around this theme. Your colleague is not as friendly anymore. One compassionate interpretation may be that she has her own troubles at the moment. A fellow student who forgets to return a book that you loaned her may be genuinely forgetful, not necessarily self-centred. The person who failed to reciprocate your generosity in the canteen may have forgotten their wallet or intend to treat you to lunch very soon. Your boss may not be friendly because possibly he does not have that type of personality. He tends to adopt the same approach to all members of the team.

If our negative thoughts are directed at ourselves, we need to exercise compassion for ourselves, too. Imagine the advice that you would give your closest friend if they were thinking the way you are thinking. Try giving yourself that same advice. If you have received a disappointing result in an exam, remind yourself that others may have as well. Maybe some of your peers are even more disappointed than you. If you were short listed for promotion but someone else gets the position, remind yourself that many others failed to make the short list and that there will be other opportunities in the future. If a friend lets you down, remind yourself that you are not a perfect friend either.

4. WEIGHING IT ALL UP

Sometimes we need to weigh up the advantages and disadvantages of our thoughts and/or our conclusions and list them out. You should continue this approach with the actions that you have planned in response to whatever has upset or angered you. Will your response make matters better or worse? Are there other alternative actions that you could consider? This exercise will prevent you from making a situation worse. Sometimes the first solution that comes to mind is not the most helpful one going forward. Deciding not to apply for a promotion ever again (because of not being successful) may mean that you will never achieve your potential within the workplace. Deciding to be unfriendly towards someone who has disappointed you may make you feel even worse or heighten your sense of alienation.

5. REDUCING YOUR VULNERABILITY TO UPSETTING THOUGHTS

Consider how to create circumstances where you would be less likely to engage in unhelpful or irrational thinking. Identify external factors and other individuals that contributed to the problem. Explaining your sensitivities to relevant people within your family, work or social circle can protect you from future periods of vulnerability. People often do not know how or why they have upset others. Discussing why certain remarks upset us may mean that those who make such remarks will refrain from doing so in the future. The teenager may have to explain to his mother that her referring solely to his poor grades in maths while ignoring successes in other subjects makes him feel dejected and angry. If you are sensitive to negative appraisal then you should refrain from asking colleagues for their views about your performance. It would even be more empowering to discover the underlying source of distress around criticism. Maybe, this emotional response is linked to an unhelpful belief system acquired as a consequence of past experience.

The truth is that we often join the dots without really knowing all the facts. We could all do with a little CBT. It's a great pity that its principles are mostly parked at the heart of a standard-ised therapy. I think CBT can potentially be utilised innovatively in schools. Wouldn't it be powerful if children learned how to step outside their emotional circle, how to make the best sense of things, how to be compassionate in their responses, how to be neutral, objective and fair-minded?

All of us are vulnerable to irrational, unhelpful and illogical thinking so it's important to work at being more rational and compassionate. Often it's not the life event that is critical but the meaning that we attach to it. The poet John Milton was more of a psychologist than he probably realised when he said, 'The mind is its own place, and in itself / Can make Heaven of Hell, a Hell out of Heaven.' I think that Milton was right. The same events or experiences do not affect people in the same way. Often our wellness or happiness is interlinked with the sense we make of ourselves, others and our world. Our own private conversations, interpretations and conclusions affect our mood and influence outcomes. It's important to become our own best friend rather than our own worst enemy in times of challenge.

While it is impossible to avoid stressful events, we can learn to hit 'pause'. We sometimes sustain stress needlessly. A huge part of stress is stressful thinking itself. The same things do not affect each of us in the same way because we sometimes think differently about them. What upsets you may not upset your friend. Indeed, we can feel annoyed with our friends for not being as annoyed as us about the same things. We're a funny lot – aren't we? We seem to look to others to validate our feelings.

Even more peculiarly, sometimes we feel that people should know how we are feeling without us even telling them. Although we humans are very intelligent, we can also be very stupid. We can assume we know things without ever finding out. I have talked to people who are angry with someone about something that they are possibly not even aware of. We are at our most vulnerable when we shut ourselves off – when we just listen to ourselves without the voice of reason being in the same room.

The Power of Questioning

Questions are very powerful tools. I regularly ask questions such as: 'Are you right to be as annoyed as you are about this? Would others be as annoyed as you? Does it matter this much? How annoyed do you want to be? How long do you want to be annoyed for? Is there another way of making sense of this? How do you know this is true? Is it helpful to be thinking this? Is it fair?'

A great deal of stress is down to how we make sense of things. We need to be more objective, neutral and logical. We need to consult more with others. Seek the evidence and then seek advice from a number of people. Don't be annoyed with people because they don't tell you what you want to hear. There is no point seeking advice if you have already decided. And be a good friend yourself – when someone asks for your opinion, tell them what you really think, not what you think they want to hear.

I will always remember one of the first clients I ever worked with. Philip suffered from depression. After a number of sessions, he interjected to say that he found my approach very helpful. He was enthused by the principles of CBT and felt that he was making steady progress. I was pleased that I was making a difference.

I reminded him at the end of one session that I was giving a public talk later that week, about how our thoughts affect our feelings and influence our behaviour – the material that enthused Philip so greatly. But his face became strained. He said, 'Where exactly is the building? Is it directly across from the cinema?' As I clarified with detailed directions he remained tense and his enthusiasm for CBT seemed to wane. 'I'd prefer not to go to that talk, if you don't mind.' When I asked why, he continued, 'I'd be afraid that people would see me going in. Everyone would know my private business.' His private business, it seemed, was that he was experiencing depression.

How we think can impact on how we behave. Philip could have potentially gained a great deal from my talk but chose to stay home. Questions that were potentially relevant to this situation were: How many people waiting in the queue for the cinema would know who he was? If there were some people who did know him in the queue, how would they know exactly what he was attending that night? And do people really care about what he might be attending?

How we think can directly affect short- and long-term outcomes. Imagine two players leaping high to catch a ball. One player is wondering whether he can catch it; he knows it's wet and slippery. It's a crucial catch at a key part in the game. He starts to doubt himself. He only hopes that he can grasp it cleanly. His opponent also sees the ball but is thinking very differently: 'Get out of my way, I'm taking this one. This is my ball.' I cannot guarantee which player will catch the ball but I know which is thinking the better thoughts.

A growing number of people are experiencing depression and thankfully many of them eventually recover. However, I would bet my last dollar that not one person who experiences recovery did not first think that recovery was possible at some stage. I have met many people who know why I cannot help them before I start. A client may be listening attentively to the therapist and nodding to affirm the effectiveness of the ongoing intervention, but privately think, 'What do you really know about depression? I see all your books on the shelves about it, but you don't have it. You don't know how I feel, so how can you help me feel better?' These private thoughts will interfere with the potential progress of that patient.

John Dewey was an eminent philosopher, psychologist and educational reformer. In the 1930s he recognised the development of an individual capable of reflective thinking as a prominent educational objective. His ideas went on to influence many other experimental models and advocates. Problem-Based Learning (PBL) is a method widely used in schools and incorporates his ideas pertaining to learning through active inquiry. Getting children to learn through active inquiry for situations encountered outside the curriculum would prove very beneficial.

Psychologist Jean Piaget asserted that the principal goal of education is to create men and women capable of doing new things, not simply repeating what other generations have done. He maintained that the educational system should produce adults who are creative, inventive and eager to discover. According to him, the next goal of education was to form minds that can be critical, can verify, and not accept everything they are offered. The ability to think independently, to step 'outside the circle', to consult before one concludes, to see the whole situation before acting, would fulfil much of his second aspiration for education.

Teaching Children the Skills of Rational Thinking

There would be massive benefits for school-going children if they were taught the skills of rational thinking. During the emotional rollercoaster of the teenage years, many students bring unnecessary stress upon themselves. I remember one student telling me that her German teacher, Miss Kavanagh, hated her guts. Even her best friend confirmed her theory. However, as I teased through the situation with her through careful questioning, we discovered that Miss Kavanagh didn't have a particularly friendly disposition towards any students. And the student finally agreed that her teacher did not hand back her copy any differently than to her peers.

I also recall another student who wanted to leave school despite her impressive grades. She told me that the reason she wanted to leave was that everyone in the school hated her. She forcefully made the point: 'I've told my parents. It's simple – everyone hates me here. Would you want to stay in a place where everyone hated you?' But as we continued the conversation she eventually smiled when I asked her if she had surveyed everyone in school – all classes, teachers, administrative staff and the caretaker. The truth is that no such survey had been conducted. With further investigation I learned that she had fallen out with two friends. Her irrational thinking was exacerbating her situation. Students will always encounter situations that justify their emotional distress but can also experience unnecessary stress and anxiety. As a former teacher I see huge potential to curb tension and possibly prevent some emotional explosions within schools through the promotion of rational thinking.

An Irrational Journey

It was a very wet day in Sligo and the roads were heavily congested. I couldn't locate a parking spot anywhere and decided to head to the shopping centre instead. I circled the indoor car park for about ten minutes. All floors were full. I just wanted a space for five minutes so that I could post a letter. I decided to try once more before surrendering to the lottery of finding a parking space on the street. Slowly, I crawled around, watching every move. Some people have a very annoying habit of approaching their car with bags but, instead of getting in their car, they open the boot, throw their bags in and walk straight back to the shops. Other people tantalise you by hanging around their car and chatting on their mobiles as if there was no tomorrow. Then there are evil people who open their doors and sit comfortably into their cars but don't switch on the ignition. It's as if they have parked in that spot just to sit there for the rest of their lives.

As I turned a corner on the second floor, I spotted a heavenly sent gap – the last parking space available. Patience is a virtue. Yes. But it was at a sharp corner and would involve serious manoeuvring to get the angle right, a major challenge even with a parking-assist bumper. I twisted and turned, withdrew and entered, stopped and started in an exercise that lasted about five minutes. I felt great satisfaction when I straightened up into the space. Parking fit for a prince.

But as I took out the key, it clicked with me that the car was inches from the wall on my side but also merely inches from its nearest neighbour on the other. Perfect parking but I couldn't leave the vehicle. If I had had a sunroof, there might have been possibilities. Just as I was making this discovery, I glanced over at the car parked directly across from me. Its driver had a bold grin on his face. It was as if he had realised my dilemma and was enjoying my plight, or was maybe watching for my next move. When we find ourselves in such ridiculous situations, the one thing we don't want is an audience.

Pride gripped me. Would I let him delight in my stupidity? Was there any other option? I decided to pretend that I was parking for a snooze and slowly lowered my seat backwards. So there. Maybe I parked knowing fully that I had no intention of getting out at all. Maybe I was just waiting on someone else. There would be no satisfaction for the glaring eyes of Mister Nosey. I snuggled into the seat and waited for him to make his exit. I waited. And waited. Stalemate. Was he sitting me out? Was he calling my bluff?

I opened one eye and spied on my subject with intensity. He was still wearing the bold grin but as I studied his face more carefully I noticed that both his eyes were closed. My enemy was simply someone having a nap in his car. Taking a genuine snooze, unlike me. Mister Nosey was not Mister Nosey at all. He hadn't even witnessed my stupidity. We all have the capacity to annoy ourselves needlessly about things that don't matter. Even psychologists.

We are thinking beings. Most of what we think is never spoken. We know that how we think affects our moods and influences outcomes. The thoughts we have about ourselves and others affect our relationship with each other. With our busy life schedules we rarely have time to think. I remember one woman telling me clearly: 'I haven't time to think. My head is spinning. I'm losing time talking to you. That's how busy I am.' But we should create space to examine how we think. Thinking about how we think would allow us to be more likely to engage in thoughts that would be productive. Becoming more emotionally aware would also allow us to realise how sometimes we cannot think straight. This may be because of what we are experiencing or have recently gone through. Consulting with others, calming ourselves down and posing good questions about our perspectives or intended actions would help us think more objectively and become more fair-minded. It's easy to stay angry for too long, to worry needlessly about things and prolong our problems because we think that they cannot be resolved. If thinking affects our mood and outcomes, then changing the way we think about things could potentially lead to very positive results for how we live our lives.

3| we need flow in our lives: at home and in the workplace

'*The best moments in our lives are not the passive, receptive, relaxing times ... The best moments usually occur if a person's body or mind is stretched to its limits in a voluntary effort to accomplish something difficult and worthwhile.*'
—Mihály Csíkszentmihályi,
Flow: The Psychology of Optimal Experience

Paul plays the piano exceptionally well. He has spent extensive hours developing his skills since childhood. His parents invested heavily in music lessons. He performed at annual school concerts and hundreds of community events. One of the most exciting memories he has is when the grand piano arrived at home. This signalled the beginning of his route to becoming a professional musician. The large room to the side of the house became a dedicated refuge for his musical endeavours – a place for him to become lost in his work. I saw him play recently and 'lost' seems an apt word for describing the process. He literally goes into his own world. His fingers dance and every few minutes his eyes open before he returns to his inner world. His mind is fully engaged. His full attention is focused on the melody, the movements of the notes, the positioning of his fingers and how his left hand stays in sync with his right. He is 'lost in the moment'. Psychologist Mihály Csíkszentmihályi (pronounced 'chick-sent-me-high') would describe this state of being as a 'state of flow'.

Christmas was always a magical time for me, especially when Santa Claus visited. We played with new toys for hours without end. Sometimes toys needed to be assembled. New board games demanded intense concentration. There never seemed to be enough hours in the day. I remember my father was noticeably frustrated with my brother and I one particular Christmas. My brother and I had found two large cardboard boxes in the garage and converted them into cars. We drew tyres, lights and number plates on the cardboard. We pushed through the bottom and, on our knees, manoeuvred our newborn vehicles around the carpet floor. My father was probably frustrated because the expensive toys we had been given lay abandoned on the floor. We were in flow with cardboard boxes. We did not need expensive toys to engage our attention. Flow could also be 'homemade'.

When my own son was around the same age, little green plastic army men, jeeps and tanks enthralled him. He had collected hundreds of these tiny soldiers over a number of months. On the landing carpet, he would spread them out and a world war would ensue. Many world wars took place during that period in his life. I used to eavesdrop and hear him make the noises of gunfire and bombs. I was fascinated by how an imaginary world can engulf a child.

One particular Saturday a war was lasting longer than normal. Soldiers had taken their positions on the banisters, landing window and door saddles, and the whole of upstairs seemed to have been invaded. I pushed past him a few times to the master bedroom, bringing laundry from there to the utility room downstairs. He was oblivious to my touch. He was completely engaged. And he would always remain that way until the last soldier fell. Then he would need to decide whether another war would begin or whether the soldiers would return to their boxes. During those wars my son had no consciousness of time. He was unaware of himself, others or the world around him. Children are experts at becoming lost in tasks. Children's lives are full of flow.

It is remarkable how many people complain of life becoming mundane and boring. When we grow up we seem to become absorbed in the roles that we feel we should fulfil. We 'settle down'. We become properly employed. We may become a wife or husband, father or mother. Passing time can creep up on us. Work can take us over. On each street or housing estate, families rise at the same time each morning, children are bundled into cars for school, dropped at the school gate; adults proceed to the workplace, have lunch (if not too busy), return home, put the dinner on, check homework, light the fire, watch television and head to bed. Often we surrender to a daily routine and possibilities for experiencing flow become limited.

The Need for Flow in Our Lives

I remember one woman describing her life to me in this way. Fionnuala said that there was no sparkle any more. She loved her husband and realised that she was blessed with four lovely children, but she felt tired and uninspired. I remember asking her whether there was anything she loved doing. She gazed at me blankly. 'Like what?' she said. I asked if she had any hobby or pastime. She explained how she no longer had time for hobbies. By the time she cooked the dinner, helped the children with their homework and settled them for bedtime, she was exhausted. Her husband worked most nights.

I then asked if she had ever had a hobby. Her eyes lit up as she started to recall her passionate love of opera. It was a passion she had completely abandoned. I knew that she'd had no children for the first four years of her marriage so I probed further by asking whether she'd had time for opera then. Her answer was that her husband had no interest in opera. She had accompanied him to rugby games instead. Often the lack of fulfilment in our lives can be down to our own decisions. Giving up hobbies or being too busy to try something new reduces opportunities for flow in our lives. It is easier to feel deprived or hard done by when we only work and sleep. It's critical for life satisfaction that we have some flow in our lives. I have often spoken with people who openly admit to me, 'I get nothing. All I do is work and more work.' And they wonder why they aren't happy!

If playing the piano is not your type of thing, this complete immersion in an experience can also occur when we play bridge, fix something in the shed or run in a race. People often experience flow when they read. All of a sudden, they realise that it is dark outside. Because they were so absorbed in their book, they didn't notice the passing of time. Flow can be experienced when people are socially engaged – when friends lose hours as they catch up on news together. These are exceptional moments. Flow comes from doing the things we love most, the things we are best at or even in doing new things – as we become 'stretched' in the new activity. 'Stretched' describes people who are internally driven and exhibiting a sense of purpose and curiosity that is autotelic. They become absorbed by the task at hand. In flow our awareness of time evaporates as we become immersed in meaningful activity.

Sadly, when we become adults many of us leave behind the

activities that made us the most happy, such as musicians no longer playing music, or artists with unfinished paintings in the attic since getting married or becoming a parent. But we need flow even more during the challenges and the crises that life poses. When we are in flow, our worries and anxieties are not in the room with us. And we all experience anxieties and worries. We would benefit greatly from 'switching the channel' sometimes. I will always remember an old man in a tiny cottage pointing to his garden and saying, 'You're a therapist, aren't you?' before continuing, 'I'll tell you where the therapy is. It's in the clay of that garden. I lose days in my garden.' This wise man spends many evenings in his kingdom. I often feel that his daily ritual of flow has served him well.

I remember sitting in a staffroom a few years ago. Two members of staff were talking openly about their annual leave. I couldn't avoid hearing what they were saying. One woman yawned and stretched out her arms, 'I literally cannot wait until my annual leave. I'm counting the days until I have eight days in a row where I do nothing.' But while she may benefit from a rest (or need it, as she was yawning!), she needed to plan her annual leave much better. Simply spending eight days on the trot doing nothing would not energise her. She needed to plan for doing things that she really loved or even trying something new. I have often heard people complain about holidays after they return home. A young man called Dominic was summarising his weekend in Barcelona to his friends: 'You know, I came home more stressed than when I left. My wife was the same. We were asking ourselves, How much did we pay for this extra stress? Never again will we go abroad with the kids.' Although children can be great sources of stress as well as love, it is important that couples negotiate some space for themselves on holidays. If Dominic wanted to see Barcelona play Real Madrid he needed to negotiate this with his wife. She could take charge of the children when he attended the match in the Nou Camp. Likewise, if his wife wanted to shop or visit museums and galleries, he could facilitate this by taking full care of the children for the hours she required.

I have met people who are exceptionally good at doing the things that they love. I know three women who attend the cinema once a week. The take turns in choosing the movie each Tuesday night. All of them admit to being refreshed afterwards. 'We look forward to Tuesdays.' said Nuala. 'We forget about our work and our worries by surrendering to fantasy.' She maintained that a two-hour movie often cleared her mind.

I remember attending an art exhibition in Sligo. The paintings were like photographs. The details, the colouring, the texture made them almost real. The artist was a silver-haired man that everyone was congratulating. I took my place in the queue to compliment him on his work. 'You must be at this for years,' I said. 'No,' he replied, 'I only started three years ago, when I retired.' He explained to me how he had joined an art club when he had stopped being a plumber. His formal education had ceased at primary level. He had never been given colouring books or crayons as a child. He had learned a trade at thirteen years of age and it had served him well. But for most of his life he had not known that he had art in him. His painting was like a new lease of life for him in his retirement. Each work of art represented hours of him being in flow. He sensed great satisfaction when each completed work was framed.

When you sit at the window in Lyon's coffee shop in Sligo you can look down on Wine Street. Across the street you see a shop named Quirkes. It was once a butcher's shop. Michael worked in it with his father. In 1988 he took it over. But if you look more closely through the window you can see that he is no longer cutting meat. Michael is now carving wood. His works of art fill the window and he is very busy. If you look even closer you can see that he doesn't wear a watch. In fact, when I chatted to him, he told me that he often didn't know what time it was. When I explained the concept of flow to him, he immediately identified with it: 'I can spend hours chiselling at a piece of wood. I have a rough idea what I want to do. But once I start it – it just happens and I stay with it until it's finished.' All the ingredients of flow are in place in his work. I often feel that education sometimes fails to connect children to work that they will truly love. I have often met people who have told me that they hate their jobs. While we all can have bad days, it's important to experience some flow in order to be reasonably satisfied in the workplace. Michael is very fortunate to have lots of flow in his work.

I have chatted with people who legislate for flow in their lives. The truth is that many people insist on doing the things they like on a regular basis. I think this enhances their life-satisfaction. Peadar takes a week off every year for Punchestown races. 'I love the races,' he says. 'For those four hours each day I forget about myself completely and feel great afterwards.' Although Ellie is a good cook, she enrolls in a different cooking course every winter. 'I just love learning new ways of cooking,' she explains. 'I pay for the course in advance to ensure that I do it. Sometimes it's too easy to sit on the couch watching television.' Alex plays golf in Strandhill every Saturday morning in the rain, hail, sleet or snow. He says thinking about Saturday mornings carries him through the week. Hilda can lose hours in her garden. She has got so good at it that colour never leaves it. She's fully in tune with the seasons. And Dee goes for a swim every day of her life. It renews and energises her. All these people (maybe without their knowledge) have lots of flow in their lives.

Csíkszentmihályi describes flow as complete immersion in an activity and has spent most of his working life researching the concept. He describes the mental state of flow as 'being completely involved in an activity for its own sake. The ego falls away. Time flies. Every action, movement and thought follows inevitably from the previous one. Your whole being is involved, and you're using your skills to the utmost.' Almost any activity can produce flow provided the relevant elements are present. Some of the activities described earlier may demand different degrees of flow, but the ingredients for total engagement are there.

Flow tends to occur with a clear set of goals that require appropriate responses. For instance, flow is very achievable when playing chess or poker. The rules and aims of the game are clear. Immediate feedback is also possible as the game progresses – we know how we are doing and what we should do next. The pianist Paul knows what notes are coming next and when the musical piece will end. Flow activities allow a person to focus on clear and compatible goals. The satisfaction comes from the chase as well as in realising the goal.

Flow in Schools

The concept of flow and the latest research into what constitutes flow and sustains it should be of particular interest and relevance to teachers. Teacher-training should incorporate strategies for cultivating an engaged learning experience in the classroom

– and offer ways to increase flow within the whole school experience. With strategies for increasing student engagement and a knowledge of the essential ingredients of flow, experienced teachers would be able to make learning more enjoyable and appropriately challenging for individual students.

When I started my career as a teacher I had special responsibility for students with learning difficulties. As an inexperienced, new recruit to the profession, I found this very challenging. Not only was I new to teaching but I had no experience whatsoever of working with children with learning difficulties. I found that they became restless easily. They would openly declare their boredom. Students with special needs were being integrated into mainstream schools at the time, but there were few or no available books or resources that suited the Irish context. I practically had to invent a curriculum for them myself. In the process, my job absorbed me.

Family and friends still remember how happy I was during those early years in teaching. I kept reinventing the wheel. I searched the world for classroom resources for children with learning difficulties and, with the help of a very supportive principal, I assembled an impressive library of tailor-made learning resources that suited their abilities and ages. Within a short number of years, education officials were encouraging even more integration of these students into the mainstream. This policy shift from special school to integration proved extremely challenging to teachers. I was often asked how I kept my students engaged and how I maintained their attention.

The secret was that the tasks I set helped them experience flow. If a child is over-challenged and the task is pitched above their ability, they become anxious and restless. If the task is pitched below their ability and is too simple, they complete it too quickly. Restlessness follows that scenario, too. It is critical to get the balance right to keep these students 'stretched'. It is difficult to arrange for flow on a regular basis within schools but the principle is exceptionally relevant when it comes to designing lesson plans.

A lack of flow experience may also be at the heart of what is perceived as disruptive behaviour. How can teachers cultivate an engaging learning experience in the classroom? What can teachers do to better hold the attention of students? How can we get students to want to learn? These are very real issues within education. When I recall my own education, I remember very little flow. I used to eagerly await the bells that signalled the end of each class. But there were occasions when the bell's ring took me by surprise. This was usually during art class.

When I was a teacher I remember one student who continually struggled with Irish. Christy was a bright boy but always displayed a dour appearance. He seemed unhappy at school. He wore that unhappiness with ease. He was prone to anger tantrums and sighed when he felt bored in class. Teachers regularly chatted among themselves about his attitude. The reality was that Christy was dyslexic. Christy's issue was never one of intelligence, but it did relate to his specific learning disability. The system favours children who can read, comprehend what they have read, learn what they have read and write it in a structured way within a set time in exams. Children with dyslexia do not always find these hurdles easy to negotiate. Christy's failing was in the final step. Due to his learning disability, he had significant difficulties in packaging what he had successfully understood and learned into structured written form, particularly against the clock. Teachers often remarked on how unhappy he looked in their classes. But of course he was unhappy! He never experienced success and all the emphasis was on his inadequacies and poor grades. His years at school were marked by a profound lack of flow.

I remember being charged with the responsibility of teaching him Irish. Even students without specific learning disabilities find Irish challenging. It can be a torturous experience for those who struggle with basic literacy skills in English. Christy was never going to be able for honours level but he failed consistently at ordinary level, too. To this day, I still remember his long face when I gave him his mark for what was his final school exam in Irish. His next exam in Irish would be a state examination. I would have loved to have given him a pass grade but I could only find 30 per cent, and that was with a generous heart. He sighed and his frustration was tangible.

When class ended I asked him to stay behind for a chat. He seemed even more disgruntled by that suggestion. During the ensuing five minutes I extracted the information that his career goal was to be a garda. A pass grade in Irish was compulsory during those years in order for him to pursue this objective. He explained openly to me about how much he hated Irish. I explained that I fully understood his situation. Failing at something the whole time does not make us like it more. However, I informed him that I was thrilled with his 30 per cent. He smiled, thinking that I was joking.

I elaborated further by stating that there were four months left to find another 10 per cent for a pass. I emphasised that I had not lost faith in him and that 30 per cent in a subject he despised and found difficult was actually impressive. I also gave him a sheet of commonly used Irish sentences that could be useful in any essay that might appear in the exam. From that day, his attitude was transformed. He was more alert in class; he asked more questions. Maybe it was hope that I had injected into his situation. If we know what is required, if we know where we are going and, crucially, if we feel that we are getting there, more flow (even in Irish class) is always possible.

Before this point, he was simply attending classes. Now his sheer determination to work towards the 40 per cent he needed changed his whole demeanour in school. I also taught the most intelligent students and they had an uncanny way of communicating that they were bored if they found what I was teaching to be unchallenging material. Children seem to have limitless curiosity and thirst for knowledge before they enter school. However, several years later, many of those same children can be found in the classroom with their minds wandering and their attention straying. Within a short time, student motivation becomes a real problem. If the flow experience is alien to them, they are more likely to drag their feet.

The Need for Flow in the Workplace

We can also experience flow in our work. The surgeon experiences flow as she performs an operation. The business entrepreneur experiences flow as he closes a new deal. The secretary experiences flow as she learns a new software package.

Sometimes the very thing we dread, i.e. change, is exactly what we need in order to increase satisfaction in the workplace. People can find themselves doing the same things for too long. They are no longer being challenged. They can almost complete these tasks in their sleep. Such jobs inevitably become boring.

A new challenge or a change in responsibility can provide more fulfilment as the employee experiences flow again. Being overly skilled at work leads to boredom and the experience of never-ending days. Being under-skilled leads to stress and anxiety. It's about getting the balance right. That's why it is so important to have clear goals, rules of performance and regular feedback to sustain a healthy work environment.

We spend a considerable amount of our lives working. When you take an average working week, and add those hours to the number of hours spent sleeping, it represents the majority of our lifetimes. Sometimes work follows us home and steals even more of our precious time. Are you happy at work? Even reasonably happy? I have spoken to many people who hate their jobs. They tell me about how their days at the office seem to never end. I will only explore the option of changing career with these people if they first attempt to make their experience of work a more positive one by asking themselves the following questions: What can be done to induce more flow into your working day? Could any tasks be surrendered or delegated to another colleague (maybe a colleague who is very keen to change responsibilities)? Are there any new responsibilities that you can volunteer for? Is there a new section or department you could consider changing to? Can you change the way you are doing things? Are there new skills that you could acquire that would lead you to do what you do more efficiently? Sometimes people can claim to be bored but have resisted anything to do with change over the years.

But change itself can sometimes be the remedy. Even a change in career can be stressful at the beginning but more rewarding as we find ourselves 'stretched' again. It is only in recent years that I have come to understand why I left my teaching post. Colleagues at the time seemed shocked that I was leaving a job in which I had achieved such high levels of competency (within special education). But that was the problem: I had conquered the skills involved. The days were getting longer. I was finding it too easy. I probably would have stayed in education longer if I had been given a completely different responsibility. If challenges are too small, one gets back to a state of flow by increasing them. If challenges are too great, one can return to the flow state by learning new skills to feel 'comfortably stretched'.

Studies have shown that there are more occasions of flow in the workplace than in our free time. Sitting aimlessly in front of a television or screen, or lying on the couch, does not encourage flow. Indeed, all the evidence suggests that free time is more difficult to enjoy than work. We waste so much time. We would never feel that we had wasted this free time if we experienced more flow when we are actually free.

Work tends to be more structured and we move from task to task during the day. Work usually has clear goals and rules of performance. Work also provides feedback in the form of knowing that we are progressing and achieving, in terms of measurable sales and better results, or in the form of affirmative words from a supervisor, colleague or client. A job also tends to encourage concentration and prevents distractions. It is a huge decision to leave the security of a permanent and pensionable position. But if it genuinely interferes with our health or makes us miserable, we need to access independent advice about options for coping better or for plotting a feasible escape route.

I know a man who has swept the streets and roads of the same town for over 50 years. I saw him in rain, hail, sleet and snow. I often felt that the poor man was stuck – that maybe limited education had restricted his options. I arranged to chat to him about his job as preparation for this book. Initially, he challenged me by asking if I was interviewing him because I thought that he was unhappy or bored in his work. He assumed that a psychologist would never explore a subject such as life happiness or job satisfaction. During our short interview, he enlightened me about how people can often be much happier than we might think.

He certainly shocked me when he declared that he worked an hour earlier in the morning unpaid. He preferred the early start, he said. He reminded me about the exercise he was getting, and how he was always chatting with members of the community. He said that he never put on weight and rarely visited a GP. He stunned me with this casual comment: 'I see the stretch in the evenings. I know when the daffodils come out and if they are earlier or later than the previous year.' He reminded me that he enjoyed being his own boss. He could start his day down at the forest or at a housing estate. He could have sought promotion years ago and we laughed as he said that if his employers knew his real age he'd have been forced to retire years ago. His entire approach to each day was so refreshing. He made each day different.

Short of making a dramatic career change, or leaving, there are many ways to make one's job produce flow. The shop assistant who decides to connect in a real and meaningful way with each customer; the nurse who deliberately monitors the progress of his patients because he wants to see them progress; the salesperson who is keen to see that customers are happy and who follows up with a call; the manager who checks on an employee following a bereavement. Connecting with people, customers or colleagues in a real and meaningful way can be energising.

It can be too easy to just turn up for work and do what is expected. Many people follow the same routine and never consider changing tasks around. But we should pay close attention to each step involved. Maybe we need to focus more on what we do and consider other ways of doing the same thing – better ways. By making a list of your responsibilities, you could contemplate whether any could be completed more effectively if you became more skilled. Then you would enjoy those tasks more, rather than experiencing anxiety around them. Maybe we could work in partnership with a colleague on improving the steps involved. Is this particular step necessary? What additional steps could make my contribution more valuable? If, instead of spending energy trying to cut corners, we put the same amount of attention into finding ways to accomplish more on the job, more efficiently, we could enjoy working more and probably be more successful.

Flow within the Home

In contrast to the work environment, people often lack a sense of purpose and direction when spending time at home with the family or alone. Often it is assumed that no skills are required to enjoy free time and that anyone can do it. But we know that sometimes a weekend of 'rest' or a fortnight's holiday does not refresh us. The evidence suggests that free time is sometimes more difficult to enjoy than work. Research indicates that leisure time in our society is occupied by three major activities: an ever-growing media consumption, conversation, and active leisure (i.e. hobbies, going out to restaurants/cinema, sports and exercise, etc.).

Not all these free-time activities produce the same flow. In a survey of American teenagers, flow was only experienced about 13 per cent of the time in front of a television, 34 per cent when performing a hobby and 44 per cent when playing a sport. However, this research also indicated that the same teenagers spend at least four times more of their free hours in front of the TV. Similar ratios were recorded for adults. To make the best of our free time, we need to devote as much planning and attention to it as we would do within the dynamics of work. Relationships can become stale because people with different interests can fall in love. If both partners share little or no interests, hobbies can often die.

Sometimes the compromise reached is to do things together whether both parties enjoy the same things or not. This would be like opera-loving Fionnuala attending rugby games with Bill. Or, alternatively, her staying at home while her partner attended the game. But there is another option – Fionnuala attending opera and Bill attending the rugby. While it's always healthy for relationships for both parties to do things together, it should not be at the expense of losing what makes us tick.

The success of gaming platforms like PlayStation and Xbox stem from their ability to induce flow in people. Children cannot leave their consoles or screens. When they are called for dinner, they scream about needing to complete a new level. They argue about how they are nearly finished and don't want to lose their progress. And accessing a new level will 'stretch' them further. However, as with most things, we have to be careful not to over-indulge. It would be detrimental to children's development if they spent all their leisure hours on the gaming consoles.

Some Tips for Increasing Flow in Your Life

Return to a Hobby

Many of us leave a hobby behind us as we grow older and settle down. It may be music, art or drama that we surrender to the responsibilities of relationships, parenting or work. Or a sport like golf or tennis that was squeezed out of our regular schedule because we no longer planned time for it. Happy people do the things they love doing more often. So return to that hobby. Dust down the piano. Join up with some other musicians. Borrow some golf clubs and join a club. Volunteer to act in a drama or put your name down to audition for a choir. We all need some space to forget about the stresses and worries of life.

Take Up a New Hobby

Starting something new has the added benefit of 'stretching' you and that sense of being stretched is a key component of being in flow. However, if you enrol for classes in sewing, pottery, a new language, or gardening, make sure that you pitch yourself at the right level. Don't join a beginner's class if you are not a beginner. You'll only be bored because the tasks involved will not sufficiently challenge you. And don't overrate your ability by joining classes aimed at more experienced or qualified members, as you will not enjoy these classes as much and will feel inadequate in comparison to the others attending, or will simply find the classes stressful. It's important that you have a good tutor who can teach you the skills needed. Learning and applying these skills will enhance the flow.

Become More Social

We can often experience great flow when we connect with people. However, many people have a very limited social circle outside of work colleagues and immediate family. We should develop social contacts with our community and avail of opportunities to get to know more people. We can experience great flow by becoming lost in conversations that remove us from our problems.

Engage with the Arts

Sometimes we forget that we don't have to be an artist to appreciate art. We do not need to be an accomplished musician to enjoy music. We don't need to be a film producer to attend the cinema. The arts can engage us and provide great flow. Our imagination is a pathway to experiencing flow. Join a film society or book club, or arrange a regular night for some arts entertainment. Ask a few friends to join you, form a habit and you will avail of the added bonus of social connectivity.

Switch Things Around at Work

If you feel that your workdays are endless, maybe it's because you experience little or no flow in them. Is it possible to switch responsibilities? Change to another skill or division? Perhaps you could volunteer to join a new group or project, or request training in a new skill and/or plan to work in a new area soon. Or maybe you need a career change and with careful planning and consultation could dramatically increase flow in your workplace.

Planning 'Golden Days'

We all work hard and life can be stressful. Many people have no flow in their lives at all. They just continue doing the things they feel that they are meant to be doing. We should plan for more flow by allocating days in our diary each month for taking time out to enjoy something we love doing. I often refer to these days as 'golden days'. Maybe each month you could earmark a day to spend at the beach or a night for the theatre. Maybe you could book your favourite restaurant and organise some friends to meet there. Life is precious and time goes by quickly.

We all need more flow in our lives. In addition to making activities more enjoyable, flow also has a number of other benefits. Research indicates that flow enhances performance in a large number of areas, including teaching, learning and artistic creativity. Because the act of achieving flow involves a strong mastery of specific skills, we need to continually seek new challenges to maintain the flow. Isn't it interesting that when we assess for depression, one of the areas measured is pleasure and a low score in pleasure is considered significant in the overall diagnosis? We need to allow for more pleasure and flow in our lives. In doing so, we will experience more happiness, and better health, too.

4| cultivating compassion

'No one has ever become poor by giving.'
—Anne Frank

One of the most attractive features in humans is their ability to be kind. Kindness as a trait is almost magnetic in its effect. It draws people closer to each other. As children, we always searched for it, particularly when we were in need. If we fell and cut our knee, we ran to a loving parent to be lifted up, hugged and attended to. We needed to experience their compassion in our moments of despair. When we entered a room of strangers, it was only when we sensed kindness from one of them that we eventually dared to glance up, acknowledge their presence and eventually speak. Sometimes it was just a kind smile from the doctor that eased the tension during a visit to the clinic. The kind teacher was always our favourite teacher.

As teenagers, we became upset when a compassionate response to our crises was not forthcoming. We wanted empathy and some flexibility from parents and siblings when we experienced friendship conflicts or romantic heartbreak. It was not just knowing that someone loved us that was important, but also feeling it. When family reached out to us in kindness, we felt that love. That feeling was always magical.

My late mother was a nurse who was full of kindness. She mothered me into my forties, worrying about me, offering advice, but essentially spoiling me with endless kindness. I miss that compassion so much now. I often felt that whoever was in her care was privileged. Her former patients and colleagues always highlight this characteristic when remembering her. She worried about her patients, monitored their progress with a caring eye, eased their anxieties and harnessed hope for them. I often remarked that it was a crucial characteristic in a happy nurse – that ability to be compassionate. She was always so happy at nursing because she was tapping into her strength – compassion.

We know that anger and hostility affects our physiology in a very dramatic way. Vengefulness towards a work colleague can keep us awake at night. As we script a row or argument for the next day, we twist and turn in our beds. Our heart races and adrenaline pumps through our system. We have an innate ability to facilitate this fight or flight response. We know how to defend and attack. It's almost a spontaneous response to challenge. There is an inner biology that facilitates this.

Some scientists have made the case that the ability to be kind and reach out to others in compassion also has a biological basis. In one study, unique activity in the region of the brain associated with positive emotion was recorded in subjects when scientists tested for a biological basis to compassion. The study conducted by psychologist Jack Nitschke at the University of Wisconsin showed how mothers, when shown photographs of numerous babies, responded differently on seeing their own child. They not only reported feeling more compassion but also demonstrated unique activity in the region of their brains associated with positive emotions. It seems to be the case that the brain is attuned to our offspring from birth.

In another study at Princeton University, when participants contemplated scenarios in which harm may be done to others, a similar response occurred in their brains. The same network of neurological regions lit up. The feelings of compassion could be mapped in the brains of the subjects. Two very different experiments provoked similar neurological reactions. Maybe compassion is an innate response within humans. The latest science suggests that just as we have an innate response to fight or take flight, we also have an innate response to be loving and compassionate.

The autonomic nervous system acts as a control centre for many of our spontaneous responses. It affects heart rate, digestion, respiratory rate, salivation, perspiration, pupillary dilation, micturition (urination) and sexual arousal. It helps regulate our blood flow and breathing patterns for different kinds of actions. If we feel threatened, this so-called 'fight or flight' response is triggered. For instance, if we were walking down a cul-de-sac and suddenly noticed an Alsatian dog barking and running towards us, we react decisively and, crucially, instantly, to our circumstances. Within seconds we find ourselves fleeing from the threat, running as fast as our legs can carry us, possibly jumping heights that we could not have believed possible. In such situations our bodies undergo a revolutionary physiological response.

The automatic nervous response system's profile for threatening situations has been mapped by science. But is there a response instigated by the same control centre for situations that require kindness and compassion? A number of scientists have shown this to be the case. The hormone oxytocin plays a critical role in sexual reproduction, in particular during and after childbirth. It facilitates the birth process, maternal bonding and the secretion of milk within the breasts. Scientists have also investigated its role in numerous other areas, including social recognition, pair-bonding and lovemaking.

Oxytocin, known as the 'love hormone', has been shown to critically promote long-term bonding and commitment among humans. It lies at the heart of compassion. Indeed, many studies have shown that it elevates when people perform behaviours associated with compassionate love. As the teacher stoops to chat more intimately to an excited child about her new shoes, the warm smiles, friendly hand gestures and loving voice tones are facilitated by the oxytocin hormone. Social psychologists have also investigated whether it can promote altruistic behaviour in humans.

One such psychologist, Daniel Batson, makes a persuasive case that it does. He has asserted that 'feeling empathy for a fellow being in need evokes motivation to help [that person] in which these benefits to self are not the ultimate goal of helping; they are unintended consequences' (Batson & Shaw, 1991: 114).

Batson is probably the strongest proponent of the theory that people often help others purely out of the goodness of their hearts. But is there science to back this? Is compassion a biological-based skill or a virtue? Is it something we are born with, or a skill that can be taught and learned? Can compassion influence health or enhance happiness?

In 2008 the UK Government Office for Science published the *Mental Capital and Wellbeing* project. This comprehensive report focused on the UK but is also relevant to the interests of other countries. Its scope was possibly unparalleled in examining the best available scientific and other evidence, and considering the factors that influence an individual's mental development and well-being from conception until death. The report provided an assessment of how the policies of key government departments, important stakeholders such as educators, healthcare professionals and employers, and an individual's specific environment, affect health outcomes. It also analysed possible interventions to address the future challenges in promoting greater health and well-being of citizens.

It concluded that one of five best ways to mental well-being was to give. This recommendation is based on the collation of scientific studies confirming that being kind is good for our health but also makes us happier.

Kindness Is its Own Reward

I remember as a young teenager being brought around homes by my father as a volunteer with the Meals on Wheels scheme. We'd collect about twenty dinners and deliver them to families that had no food in their fridges. The poverty I witnessed brought me out of my own comfort zone. My dad used to say, 'It's nice to be nice, son,' but it is only in recent years that I have discovered that it is also good for you. There is no doubt that when we commit an act of kindness we feel good afterwards. It is so easy to get locked into our own world and see our problems as the only ones that exist. Sometimes we want exclusive rights to stress. We can convince ourselves that we have the worst problems in the world. Helping others not only protects us from becoming self-obsessed but can also be a great help to ourselves in contextualising our own problems.

On a spiritual level we may feel that kind acts are the right thing to do because deep inside we know this world is not all about ourselves. We may feel that something profound and deep within points us towards a belief that this is what we are meant to do – reach out to those in need. We may also feel that such acts give our lives meaning and purpose. But the 'feel-good factor' that follows an act of compassion may be explained solely on a biochemical level. Some recent science suggests that its basis lies in the fact that the brain's natural versions of morphine and heroin, which we know as endogenous opioids, trigger elevated levels of dopamine to produce a 'helper's high' effect.

Scientist David Hamilton has focused his attention on this so-called physiology of kindness. He makes the case that kindness can be said to be cardio-protective – good for the heart. In an interesting study, outpatient cardiac patients who made regular visits to support inpatient cardiac patients were shown to have a heightened sense of purpose and reduced levels of despair and depression.

Kindness seems to be its own reward. A study by Maria Pagano and colleagues at Brown University Medical School involving participants in the Alcoholics Anonymous programme examined the relationship between helping other alcoholics to recover and incidences of relapse in the year following treatment. The twelfth step of the programme facilitates the sober alcoholic remaining with the group to encourage and inspire others still suffering from their addiction. Not everyone completes this twelfth step. But those who do seem to experience better outcomes.

The study found that recovering alcoholics who helped other alcoholics were significantly less likely to relapse in the year following treatment. Among those who helped other alcoholics (8 per cent of the study population), 40 per cent successfully avoided alcohol in the year following treatment, compared to 22 per cent of those unengaged in helping others to recover. In a study by C.E. Schwartz, a group of people with multiple sclerosis volunteered to help fellow sufferers despite their own significant symptoms. Over two years, the volunteers showed pronounced improvement in self-confidence, self-esteem, depression and role functioning. They especially benefited in terms of protection against depression and anxiety. Hamilton reminds us that such acts elevate our levels of oxytocin. He explains that oxytocin causes the release of a chemical called nitric oxide, which dilates (expands) the blood vessels. The hormone is known as a 'cardio-protective' because it protects the heart by lowering blood pressure.

He has also written about how kindness potentially slows aging. The increase in oxytocin reduces levels of free radicals and inflammation in the cardiovascular system and thus slows aging at its source. Incidentally, these two culprits also play a major role in heart disease, so this is another reason why kindness is good for the heart.

There have also been suggestions in the scientific journals of the strong link between compassion and the activity of the vagus nerve. The vagus nerve, in addition to regulating heart rate, controls inflammation levels in the body in what is known as the inflammatory reflex. There has always been ample funding (particularly from drug companies) to scientifically prove the benefits of anti-depressants as a treatment for depression. There is no dispute about their effectiveness for many mental health disorders but this does not take away from the fact that there is a tendency to overprescribe, particularly when practitioners have such a restricted menu of scientifically validated options. Alternative and complementary treatments have received less scientific attention. It is a welcome development that increasingly non-chemical interventions have fallen under the close scrutiny of scientists. One such intervention, namely practising kindness, seems to have a positive chemical effect on our bodies.

Compassionate Meditation

There has been major growth in the practice of mindfulness, which has been shown to calm the mind, improve our ability to focus and induce an inner peace. Recent studies have suggested that it may also impact on physiological pathways that are modulated by stress and relevant to disease. There is less known about meditation practices that foster compassion. One major study at Emory University School of Medicine focused on Tibetan Buddhist compassionate meditation and found that kindness and compassion did, in fact, reduce inflammation in the body, mostly likely due to its effects on the vagus nerve.

The data suggested that engagement in compassionate meditation may reduce stress-induced immune and behavioural responses, although future studies are required to determine whether meditation techniques are more likely to exhibit reduced stress reactivity. Dr Richard Davidson is one of the world's top researchers in this field. He has studied the brains of meditators and his findings confirm that meditation seems to strengthen connections and functioning in those parts of the brain that calm feelings such as fear or anger. When he studied the brain waves of an experienced meditator, he found the highest level of activity ever seen in brain areas associated with happiness and positive emotions.

In general, research suggests that meditation supports the development of positive emotions. And preliminary research findings point towards meditation of loving kindness and compassion being associated with feelings of happiness. Mindfulness is the ultimate exercise of self-compassion.

I remember visiting a school once to give a talk to the staff. I had spoken about the health benefits of practising kindness and was chatting over a cup of tea with the newly appointed principal. He was enthused by my presentation and mentioned that six students from fourth year had worked on the missions the previous year for four weeks of their summer. I was impressed by their generosity of heart and asked if they had spoken to other students of their experience. Had they shared their photographs? Had they been commended by staff for their good work? Although the principal had shown a keen interest in their work, he needed to praise and affirm their efforts. By sharing their experiences with other students in the school, these students could potentially inspire similar acts of kindness and generosity from their peers.

It is important to cultivate compassion in young people, particularly when we have learned that it helps them as well as invariably encouraging a more compassionate ethos within our learning institutions. The first-year student who decides on her first day at school to push her wheelchair-bound peer around and continues this supportive role for six years has a big heart. The older student making conversation with an isolated and upset younger student is displaying kindness. The student who notices and brings a lost visitor to the secretary's office should be commended. These acts of kindness need to be affirmed by teachers. Critically, they also need to be fostered within the home.

Home is the landscape in which the seeds of future wellness and contentment can be sown. Within the family, children need to witness kindness in order to learn it. Far too often parents tell their children what is right or wrong. The more effective means of communicating is through demonstration. With the advent of social media and technological entertainment, children have possibly become more inward. They need to be brought to visit the bereaved neighbour by their parents. They need to accompany parents on visits to their lonely nana, their less-able grandfather, or on volunteering activities with community groups. I remember overhearing a ten-year-old arguing with his mother. She was trying to coax him to come with her to her mother's house. He reluctantly agreed but exploded when she suggested that they might stay overnight. 'No way, she doesn't even have satellite TV!' He then started to bargain and asked if he could bring his PlayStation with him.

This young boy needed to be told that the visit to his nana's house was not about him. It was about her. He needed to learn that sometimes it is important to watch Nana's television programmes with her, keep her company, put the kettle on for her and chat with her. He needed to experience this kind of visit. Otherwise he would end up on his PlayStation for hours while his mother and grandmother chatted. How would he discover the satisfaction and rewarding feeling that follows from putting others' needs first?

Volunteering helps connect us to other people. It helps us remove ourselves from our own troubles. We shouldn't pretend that we don't experience genuine challenges in life, but we shouldn't allow ourselves to become absorbed by them to the exclusion of others. Our hurt and pain need expression. We need to be heard, loved and supported, but by reaching out to others (even if it is the last thing we feel like doing) we may give ourselves a little boost in our dark moments. In a large American study, initiated in 1986, the National Institute of Aging investigated the mental and physical health of thousands of participants who volunteered their time to help within their communities. They also monitored the health of participants within the study who did not volunteer. When surveyed at four different time intervals, 1986, 1989, 1994 and 2006, the group that offered its time to help others was shown to have better mental and physical health.

Researcher Allan Luks is a renowned expert on volunteerism and how helping others can potentially benefit our emotions and physical health. He has written extensively about how volunteering helps the volunteer as well as the recipient. The volunteering adolescent has been shown to have enhanced social competency and self-esteem and also to be protected against anti-social behaviours and substance abuse (Allen *et al.*, 1997). Adolescents, particularly boys, who give have a reduced risk of depression and suicide (Benson *et al.*, 2007). Structured volunteering programmes have been incorporated into the intervention plans of long-time users of psychiatric services in many states across the US. In an era where care is being provided within community settings rather than solely within institutions, patients are connecting in an authentic and meaningful way with their fellow citizens. And this activity is lifting the mood of all concerned.

Joining a helping organisation will introduce us to new people and provide a greater degree of social connectedness. But it may also help us to remove ourselves from our own world and see into the hearts of others. All the evidence suggests that we are reinvigorated through helping other people. Volunteering should formally become part of the curriculum within education settings. We would never learn how wonderful music is if we didn't have to sing in primary school. We would never discover the engaging world of art if we were not given crayons and colouring books. The same applies to compassion. Children cannot understand it or experience its benefits unless they are facilitated with opportunities to practise it. We need to legislate for it in our own lives.

I spoke with David, a retired psychologist. He told me how he dedicated a certain amount of hours each week to taking calls for the Samaritans. I assumed that this was one activity he engaged in to occupy himself in his retirement or maintain his valuable, acquired skills as an experienced mental health professional and not allow them to become obsolete. But he told me that he had been a volunteer with the Samaritans for over 40 years. It was important, he said, to give something back.

Children need to witness compassion within the dynamics of the family. There can often be tension and indeed verbal aggression even between the most loving and caring couple. We all have the capacity to annoy each other at times. Children make themselves scarce or can be chased to their bedrooms when a row becomes louder and more vicious. Hurtful words, sarcastic remarks or uncustomary bad language may have been overheard by an eavesdropping audience. Reconciliation often takes place as the children sleep. I think it is vital that children witness the apologies, and be reminded that the behaviour was unacceptable and that forgiveness was sought and received. They need to learn that there is a value to forgiveness and that compassion accommodates this virtue.

Likewise, siblings need to learn how to empathise with each other from early on – to be able to place themselves in the shoes of their brother or sister whose favourite toy was broken, to engage in conversations with Mam and Dad about how disappointed their sister is with her exam results, or how heartbroken their older brother is after a romantic break-up. They need to learn to notice other people's hurts and wounds. They need to learn that helping the situation may mean surrendering their favourite seat, offering the last handful of chips from the bowl, or offering access to their favourite books, as such acts may comfort their brother or sister during a vulnerable period. Parents should never miss an opportunity to reinforce this empathy and kindness.

Compassion is the same whether we direct it towards others or ourselves. Remarkably, we tend to be much better at directing it at others. Whenever I talk about this subject, I always start with examples of compassion directed towards others because I want people to understand the concept first. I am always acutely aware that this is the initial step to helping them direct it to themselves. As a psychologist, I have been privileged to talk to very vulnerable people who have lost their way in life. These people encountered challenges and crises and have taken a mental health hit. They found themselves in darkness and wondered if there would see the light again. From a mental health perspective, they were suffering symptoms of depression, anxiety or stress.

Without a single exception, all of these people had a story to tell. They didn't wake up suddenly one morning with depression or anxiety. They had been slipping into it for a long time. There was one common dominator – as the main character of their own stories, they tended to hammer themselves. They blamed themselves for their plights. They explained how weak they had always been. They explained how they had caused all this harm themselves. They should have known better. They would never learn. Whatever they touched in life, it always turned to ruin. Whatever deck of cards they had been dealt, it only led them from crisis to crisis.

I was always moved by their stories, but it was even more emotional to witness how human beings can torture themselves with their own theories. Sometimes people fall into the trap of expecting a perfect life (which no one lives), a perfect family, perfect friends and colleagues. The reality is that, even if we are responsible for some of our failures, we are all imperfect and we all make mistakes. We share this truth with every human being on the planet. But not everyone hammers themselves so harshly after a failing. The people I was trying to help had no compassion for themselves at all.

We could debate whether this was due to their personality type, genetic predisposition to negative appraisals, or indeed learned helplessness, but the important point is that compassion was absent from their self-appraisals. They all had a tendency to ignore their successes or not to recognise their strengths or, crucially, to not accept that their failures are part of the human condition, and their life difficulties part of the journey. They needed to focus more on feeling connected with others, rather than isolating and alienating themselves through their sufferings.

In an often tedious and slow process, I tried to instil this compassion in them. When they contemplated the reality of their common humanity, and worked at being more objective, fair and rational in how they made sense of life events, a chink of light entered their darkness.

I was once asked to address a group of nearly 400 indebted people. It was the scariest room I have ever entered. These were people who were being pushed out of their homes by the banks – farmers losing their farms and business owners being closed down. There was a stony silence. Snow-white faces. I was deeply intimidated and asked myself whether my words could possibly reach them. I gave the best talk I could in the circumstances, but it wasn't until later that evening that I realised that the chief benefit my audience had taken from the event was not from my presentation. It was meeting other people like themselves. There was a buzz in the room afterwards as they exchanged stories and empathised with each other. The truth is that whatever challenge we have experienced, we don't have to walk far to find someone who has experienced something even more challenging.

A number of years ago my mother was given a terminal diagnosis. It was shattering news for all her family. It really knocked me back. I felt that she had just started to turn the corner after my father's death seven years earlier. Her health dramatically declined over the course of one year. I found it exceptionally challenging trying to balance my busy work schedule with my desire to visit her as often as I could. I found it to be a daunting task to foster hope in her company. All the experts and my own research indicated that her particular cancer was incurable.

I was not sleeping well. I was more irritable than usual. At times, my concentration weakened as I contemplated the reality of her pending death. But all of these symptoms were normal expressions of a deeply hurtful and anguishing experience. I am not made of stone and, like every other human being, I was vulnerable and weak.

However, I was acutely aware of this reality. I deliberately set out to 'mind' myself during this time. I was driving around Ireland visiting school and community groups. There was a deepening recession and there was no post for a psychologist within the vicinity of our homes. There were times when I was emotional and stressed. There were times when I did not feel like going out socially with my family or friends. But I was able to step outside the circle and acknowledge this reality. I made sure to talk openly about the times that I felt emotional and vulnerable: it is very important to give a voice to our feelings. I accepted love and care from those who loved me. I opened my ears to their advice. I reminded myself that when we are stressed or anxious, we need to work harder at relaxing and becoming calmer.

I was so fortunate that my experience of helping people in similar circumstances could now be applied to my own. I listened to music more. I walked more regularly on the beaches of Rosses Point and Strandhill, where I found a deep spiritual calmness. I started to pray again, hoping that prayer might help me through the challenge of losing my mother. So I knew how I was feeling. But a lot of people I have met professionally are sometimes not aware of what they are feeling. They have no language to describe their emotions. They tend to weather the storm, to carry on regardless and to let their whole world fall down on top of them.

As a former teacher I know that there is huge potential in helping children understand their emotions and teaching them coping skills. We all need to apply more self-compassion. In the inevitable challenges of life we need to stop and take closer note of our own suffering. Many of us become engulfed by our pain and can think of nothing else. But many times we also fail to acknowledge our painful reality.

Science is suggesting that the ability to be compassionate is within everyone. Some of us may find it easier to practise, for various reasons. But we all can cultivate this compassion. With practice we can get better at it. It is good for us as well as the recipient and, the more compassion we practise, the warmer and more caring our communities will become. There is a physiology to compassionate thoughts and actions. We should encourage it in our children by focusing their attention on the needs of others and, where appropriate, reaching out to help. We also need to practise compassion on ourselves. Focusing only on our imperfections, weakness and failures locks us into our own world.

Tips for More Self-Compassion

- How we translate failure is critical. Start seeing your failures as temporary setbacks.
- Embrace your imperfection as something you share with every human being on the planet.
- Accept the reality that none of us has total control over everything.
- Consider what you have in common with your fellow human beings – vulnerability.
- Remind yourself how you'd treat a good friend after failing or being rejected. Give yourself some of that same sympathy.
- Have some compassionate phrases ready for the tough times, e.g. 'This is a moment of suffering. Suffering is part of life. I need to mind myself.'

- Learn how to meditate. Learn how to calm yourself down.

- Step outside your circle. Remove yourself from the noise of life even for an hour and do something that will 'lift' your spirits or soothe you. You are entitled to do things that you love doing despite the challenges that you encounter.

- Accept the love and support offered by others as a gift, not an intrusion.

- Remind yourself that life is precious and time is passing. Whatever crisis you are experiencing now will be something you look back on later.

5| practising gratitude

'True happiness is to enjoy the present, without anxious dependence upon the future, not to amuse ourselves with either hopes or fears but to rest satisfied with what we have, which is sufficient, for he that is so wants nothing. The greatest blessings of mankind are within us and within our reach. A wise man is content with his lot, whatever it may be, without wishing for what he has not.'

—Seneca

J amsie lives in a tiny cottage up a narrow lane in the middle of nowhere. When I pushed the door open, the smoke from the pot-bellied stove caught me in the throat. The low ceiling, small boxed windows and ticking grandfather clock reminded me that I was about to meet a man from a different generation. There was a picture of Jesus and a red flickering bulb below, paying homage. The floor was a carpet of cement that ran into the two bedrooms. The room we sat in was the only reception area. Over a cup of tea we chatted about my work. He gave me a tour of his palace by pointing with beaming pride at his prized possessions – the mantle clock, the two antique china dogs at either side, the handmade rug from the early 1900s, the old leather-bound books, the silver spoons, and a painting by a cousin of his that was featured in a book about great Irish artists. He smiled as he boasted about his intelligent dog that slept beside the warm stove.

Jamsie came across as a happy man. I wanted to know

whether he was a happier man now as he approached the life landmark of 80 years. He reminded me that he had lost his wife sixteen years previously. That had knocked him back. She was his greatest friend, he said, and one never fully gets over such a loss. His two sons had settled abroad and he had bouts of loneliness but when I pressed him he was adamant that he was happy with his life: 'I'm as happy as you could possibly be. I found a lovely woman and she proved to be the greatest wife and mother. I am blessed with two wonderful sons and they are healthy and happy. I have all I need here,' he explained. 'It might look very little to you but my house is warm and cosy and the fridge is full. I want for nothing and everything you see is mine. I don't owe a penny.' He continued, 'I never felt the need to buy things that were unnecessary.' He reassured me that he was not mean. He would prefer to give a little to someone in need rather than buy something that he could do without.

Aileen is 33 years old. She fell in love with Tony eight years earlier and looks after her twin boys while he farms the land. They have a small diary farm and their income is up and down. But she's happy. She tastefully decorated the bungalow and put in a new kitchen a few months ago. She is blessed with Tony and her boys, Ruairí and Seán. She tells me that this is one of the happiest chapters in her life. When I asked about her happiness, her responses were spontaneous and deeply authentic. There was liveliness in her voice.

Then she startled me by saying, 'I am very fortunate because I have no mortgage or rent to pay.' She explained, 'All my friends have bigger and fancier houses but this is mine.' She avoided the temptation to take a loan and make it bigger and better: 'I could easily have borrowed and extended this house, added a double garage or a conservatory, but I'm happy with it as it is.'

It was her husband's parents' home and Aileen saw it as a gift. In the current recession, there are literally thousands of people who endlessly upgraded their homes or who built a property portfolio. They now face crippling debts. Jamsie and Aileen were acutely aware of what they already had, and never felt the need to seek more than that. They were deeply grateful for their lives.

What Is Gratitude?

Gratitude has been the subject of discourse among theologians and moral philosophers for centuries. Cicero declared gratitude as not only the greatest of virtues, but the parent of all the others. It seems a very straightforward emotion – a feeling of appreciation on receipt of a gift or good fortune. Dr Robert Emmons at the University of California is a leading researcher in the field. He describes gratitude as having two stages. The first is when something positive in one's life is acknowledged. Whether it is the receipt of a material gift (the mortgage-free house, in Aileen's case) or an immaterial experience (such as watching the sea returning to the sands), a categorical acknowledgment of the gift is experienced.

Emmons describes the second stage of gratitude as an understanding that the source of the gift or positive experience is outside oneself. This sense of thankfulness epitomises gratitude in its fullest sense. Emmons formally defines gratitude as 'a felt sense of wonder, thankfulness and appreciation of life'. He maintains that it runs much deeper, however, asserting that it is a more complex phenomenon with a critical role in human happiness. Growing research indicates that the practice of gratitude benefits general well-being. Studies confirm that people who keep a daily or weekly gratitude journal report fewer physical symptoms, greater optimism, more positive emotions, higher levels of attention and more exercise compared to people who recorded neutral life events or stressors (Emmons and Crumpler, 2000).

The literature on gratitude describes it in a variety of ways. Gratitude has been understood as an attitude or emotion, and adherents to the positive psychology movement define it as a human strength (Emmons and McCullough, 2003; Peterson and Seligman, 2004). Researchers from the area of positive psychology, through its empirical exploration of character strengths and its efforts to classify them, categorise gratitude as a human strength. Someone with the strength of gratitude habitually displays an appreciation of life, acknowledges what they have received from others and experiences and expresses thanks by nature. There is no need for someone with this strength to be prompted about the positives in his world. He seems to have a grateful disposition already. Many of us only experience gratitude when reminded of our good fortune, but someone with the strength of gratitude never underestimates the gifts bestowed on him. It may be the oxygen in his lungs, the health of his child or the warm breeze on his face. All are gifts to be thankful for.

In partnership with fellow psychologist Mike McCullough of the University of Miami, Emmons embarked on a series of studies showing that when people regularly and systematically cultivate gratitude, they experience a variety of psychological, physical and interpersonal benefits. Even if you consider Jamsie and Aileen to be exceptional people with a non-typical sense of gratitude about their life circumstances, studies show that gratitude can be cultivated and that health benefits are derived from such strategies. If it's good for our health then we need to learn more about it and consider incorporating the practice into our lives.

Gratitude as an Antidote to Depression

Depression affects millions of people worldwide. It has been a common human experience for centuries, variously documented and labelled. Historians have found reference to melancholia in ancient Greece. In modern times, we fully recognise it as a very real condition with significant disabling effects on the quality of life of people who suffer from it. Those who experience depression will tell you that it's not just about feeling 'down' and that it's impossible to 'snap out' of it. Many factors have been shown to contribute to the onset of depression, including genetics, changes in hormone levels, certain medical conditions, stress or grief or difficult life circumstances. The World Health Organization characterises it as one of the most disabling disorders in the world.

Talking therapy has been shown to be a powerful treatment of depression. Many studies have shown that combining depression medicine with therapy can be particularly effective. For instance, a large-scale trial involving more than 400 patients with treatment-resistant depression found that the use of Cognitive Behavioural Therapy alongside depression medication significantly reduced symptoms of depression in a study at the University of Bristol in 2013.

But what should the therapist and someone with depression be talking about? If the therapist has a CBT perspective, the conversation might revolve around past experiences, dormant belief systems, self-constructed theories, unhelpful thinking mechanisms, the connection between thoughts, mood and behaviour, and so on. If the therapist has a more psycho-dynamic approach, they may try to uncover drives and forces within the person with a particular reference to the 'unconscious', and such material may colour the conversation.

Facilitating Gratitude Exercises within Therapy

New research highlights the benefits of incorporating gratitude-building exercises within the therapy session. These studies suggest that therapists should be helping depressed clients focus on what is positive about their lives and to try and count their blessings. Such exercises reduce depressive symptoms. Research has shown that individuals who kept a journal for one week in which they recorded three things that went well each day and their beliefs about what caused the positive event reported significantly fewer symptoms of depression and significantly higher levels of happiness for six months (Seligman, Steen, Park and Peterson, 2005). The beneficial effects for subjects practising the three good things exercise became evident after one month and these benefits were sustained over three- and six-month interval assessments. Although only instructed to practise the exercise for one week, those participants who adhered to the strategy scored highest for happiness gains in the long term. Cultivating a gratitude habit, it seems, would benefit us all.

We know that people with depression have an extreme negative bias in how they process their world. This is not by choice. Their inner biology ferments and fosters this negative processing. In such circumstances, it is understandable that gratitude exercises would be very challenging – almost like the 'wrong' medicine. But including a brief count-your-blessings exercise within the therapeutic session and, more importantly, sustaining such exercises between sessions, may promote cracks in their negative constructs.

I remember attempting to introduce such an exercise for the first time with James. He was quite resistant. He sought clarification from me about the relevance of such an exercise in his current circumstances. He told me that there was nothing right about his life at that time. 'How could anything be right about my life when I have this?' he asked, referring to his depression.

I asked him to write down three things that are 'right' in his life so that we could talk about them in the next session. He maintained his stance: 'There is *nothing* right in my life.' But I interjected to ask about his eighteen-month-old daughter. What was her name? Who did she look like? Was she healthy? He got the point. Although he wasn't feeling well there were many positive things about his life that he had forgotten about. The truth was that James and I had a project to work on: his depression. This would involve serious effort and patience on his part. But there were many positive aspects to his life and he needed to remind himself of this reality. Over a number of weeks he found these exercises easier to complete. Through them we legislated for positives in his world, despite his depression. This allowed some light to shine in.

The Benefits of Practising Gratitude

By practising gratitude we develop an appreciation of what is valuable and meaningful in our lives. We encompass a state of thankfulness and/or appreciation. Experiencing gratitude, thankfulness and appreciation fosters positive feelings even in people who are not experiencing depression. Such positive feelings, if sustained, can contribute to a person's sense of well-being.

Emmons and McCullough's landmark studies on the benefits of practising gratitude examined gratitude under three experimental conditions. They divided participants into three groups. The first group was asked to record negative events or annoyances that they experienced. The second group was asked to document the things for which they were grateful, and the third group wrote about neutral life events. They continued to do this either daily or weekly for ten weeks. Across the various study conditions, the gratitude subsample consistently evidenced higher well-being in comparison to the other two study groups.

A study by Jeffrey J. Froh, Sefick and Emmons, which focused on early adolescents, similarly revealed that gratitude is associated with greater life satisfaction. Their conclusion was that being grateful enhanced self-reported gratitude, optimism, life satisfaction and decreased negative affect (mood). Their findings suggest that exercises like counting blessings act as an effective intervention for enhancing well-being in adolescents. A.M. Wood and colleagues examined gratitude and well-being in the context of personality style in another study in 2008. They concluded that gratitude had a unique relationship with life satisfaction. In another study by Wood, higher levels of gratitude predicted better subjective sleep quality and duration.

Professor N.M. Lambert at the University of Utah has conducted extensive research on relationships. He has examined how gratitude can improve them. This study of couples found that individuals who took time to express gratitude for their partner not only felt more positive towards their partner but also more comfortable about expressing concerns about their relationships, suggesting that gratitude can make a relationship healthier.

Research into marital relationships has shown that thriving relationships have and maintain a high ratio of positive to negative emotion. Renowned couple therapist J.M. Gottman maintains that by regularly expressing gratitude, we allow this positive ratio to not only develop but to become more sustainable. In 2012 Amie M. Gordon and colleagues at Universities of California and Toronto showed that people who feel more appreciated by their romantic partners reported being more appreciative of their partners. In turn, people who are more appreciative of their partners were shown to be more responsive to their partners' needs. They were also found to be more committed and more likely to remain in their relationships over time.

Curbing Envy with Gratitude

Working at being more grateful could also counteract our tendency to be envious. We do not usually vocalise envy. It burns us from inside. The only time we might let envy have its voice is when we are in the company of someone equally as envious of the same person. Then we can start belittling and denigrating the innocent party.

What is at issue is that we desire what the privileged person possesses because we feel inferior. The circumstances in which we might become envious usually involve some form of social comparison. It's as if we subconsciously measure our self-worth by using other people as a barometer. Our self-evaluation is based on what we do not possess instead of a deeper awareness of what we are blessed with. Envy grips us when we feel that we fall short in comparison to others.

Thoughts and feelings of envy can lead us to develop animosity towards an individual and anguish within ourselves. If we press pause and focus on our blessings, we might reduce our comparisons to others. If we work at building a purposeful appreciation for what we already have, we might experience more inner contentment rather than a constant longing for what we do not have. Too many people spend their lives trying to become someone else instead of embracing the wonderful person they already are.

Curbing our Negative Bias with Gratitude

People often spend too much of their valuable energy vividly dwelling on what has gone wrong in their lives. But life has been kind to us all. Practising gratitude has been shown to make it easier for us to remember positive experiences because when we sense gratitude, our happy memories (and we have all experienced good times) act as an antidote to a negative recall bias. By practising gratitude we may potentially develop a more positive frame of mind.

I went to a very enjoyable family wedding in Bordeaux a few years ago. Most of the wedding party stayed for a week. Whenever the family gathers and recalls those special days, the sense of gratitude that we feel for the success of the event allows an abundance of memories to flow into our conversation. It's as if Bordeaux awakes from its sleep within our memories.

But how can we nurture more gratitude in our lives? In his book *How to Want What You Have*, Timothy Miller suggests four different routes to nurturing a greater awareness of gratitude in one's life: (1) identify non-grateful thoughts; (2) formulate gratitude, i.e. supporting thoughts; (3) substitute the gratitude-supporting thoughts for the non-grateful thoughts; and (4) translate the inner feelings into outward actions. He maintains that by following these steps, a person can live with greater contentment.

I prefer a simple count-your-blessings exercise, and a good time to do this is before you fall asleep at night. Make a concentrated effort to remember some of the best moments from the day before it ends, and take them to sleep with you. Once we begin these kind of exercises, it is remarkably easy to build on them and experience a deeper sense of satisfaction. It's all about beginning.

Barriers to Gratitude

Sometimes, due to our mood, we may not even like being reminded about the positives. It seems that gratitude does not come naturally to everyone. I have previously referred to a negative bias in how humans process information. Scientists believe that our minds are skewed to process stimuli as threats rather than gifts. We have possibly survived as a species because of this bias – eradicating all other threats since the beginning of time. But this bias does get in the way of gratitude.

I remember overhearing a conversation between two shop assistants in a local stationery shop. Schools were about to close for the summer and the customer had enquired about a 'Thank You Teacher' card. They were scathing in their whisperings: 'Teachers are paid to do their jobs. What do they need thank-you cards for?' I have met nurses who feel that the more they do for their patients, the more that is expected of them. An attitude of entitlement can impair our ability to initiate feelings of gratitude. Just because the inspirational teacher is paid to teach or a compassionate nurse enjoys a salary for her work does not mean that we should not appreciate their efforts. Expressing gratitude to people who help and support us affirms and encourages them in their work. It also has a positive effect on us by awakening us to how gifted we are to have these people in our lives.

Pessimism is another factor that interferes. Some people have a well-formed habit of only seeing the negative, predicting bad outcomes instead of positive, fostering suspicion when people offer kindness, and dedicating themselves to analysing the causes of all their problems. Science has shown that pessimistic thinking can predict depression (Gillham and Reivich, 2004; Nolen-Hoeksema, 2000).

I remember encountering one man, Alex, who was engulfed by his own pessimism. It was understandable because he had just experienced a very traumatic change in his life circumstances. Alex had worked hard to become a successful businessman. He exemplified the Celtic Tiger during the boom years: Work hard and you'll be successful, and then you'll be happy. At one stage he employed 23 people in the building-supplies sector. People used to slow down to peer through the thick hedge when they passed his mansion. His children went to fee-paying schools. His wife drove a jeep. From a very ordinary and humble rural background, an extraordinary entrepreneur was born. Alex treated his staff well and was a pillar of his community. He was generous and sponsored many local community initiatives. He was particularly open-minded about hiring people with disabilities and was convinced that with adequate training they could make a real and meaningful contribution to the workplace. Alex was a successful man, but also a good man.

He took advice from financial consultants during the Celtic Tiger years. In retrospect, that advice was bad advice. He was one of the many business people who fell victim to the economic collapse. His buildings were all for sale. The building sector crumbled and all of his money was tangled up in it. His customer base evaporated. He owed money that he would never be able to repay. The bank repossessed the mansion.

Over a number of months, he began to feel unwell; his sleep became disrupted; he lost considerable weight. Tension increased in his relationship with his wife, Helena. They became too stressed to help each other when that was exactly what they needed to do. In times of challenge we have to tap into our own resources. But Alex seemed to have surrendered. He was slipping into a deep depression, engulfed by a profound sense of hopelessness. He told me that his life was shattered and the future was a blur.

There are so many frightened people as a consequence of the recession – people lost in a fog of economic turmoil and uncertainty. My heart goes out to Alex and people like him. Maybe he made mistakes. Maybe he should have known better. Possibly he simply became tempted. Having lots of money sometimes makes us want to have even more. But Alex was a good person. He was deeply loved by his wife and two daughters. He was approaching 60 and was probably beginning to tire anyway. Running a business is hard work. He mentioned to me that he regretted not really knowing his teenagers as they were growing up. He was too busy. Maybe he was lost long before the recession.

When Alex was telling me about his demise, he said something that threw me – 'Living over my father's pub is humiliating and soul-destroying. I am such a failure.' I realised I had assumed that he was in rented accommodation. Alex had *not* lost everything, after all. His elderly father had invited him back into the family business. He was gifted with a rescue plan. Alex still had a beautiful and healthy wife. She loved and needed him. He had two gorgeous daughters, both of them now working in Ireland, at a time when so many young people were emigrating. Was it not wonderful that his generous father held on to his pub and house during the recession, and was so welcoming?

It also meant that a new project was right under Alex's nose. He had always loved new projects. Could he get the crowds back into the pub? What about food? Helena was a great cook and had always talked about running a coffee shop. Maybe she had a project under her nose, too. There was no doubt that a chapter had closed in the book of Alex and Helena's life, but maybe they would have more time for each other now. He could make up for the lost teenage years and get to know his daughters as the beautiful and successful women they had become. And remember: Alex *had* tasted financial success. Many people only dream of such success and never come close to knowing what it's like. Maybe it was time to slow down a little and get in touch with his inner self, and start living again.

When we encounter crisis, we have to dig deep. We can easily spend all our energy talking about what we have lost, or listing out what we need. By parking ourselves in the past or planting ourselves into the future, we can blind ourselves to the gift of 'now'. Things would never be the same again for Alex. But he could only pay the bank what he could pay the bank. That's the way it works. He still had a life to live. This new chapter in his life could be one of the best chapters ever. Often when we find ourselves back where we started, we see the world differently and can make more room for what really matters. Some would say that it is only when we think we have lost everything that we truly find ourselves.

Advising Alex to cultivate a sense of gratitude is something he might not have appreciated. However, if he could consider the positives about his life, his mood could improve. In the cases of Aileen and Jamsie, both could emphatically see how fortunate their circumstances were. Jamsie had lost his wife and his two sons had emigrated, but he was happy with what he still had. Aileen appreciated that her marriage was practically immune from financial stress. She was aware of her privileged position. Alex's world had crumbled all around him and gratitude was something he could not contemplate at that juncture.

A deep sense of insecurity and disempowerment was felt by thousands of people in Ireland due to the economic downturn. The future can seem bleak, and it is easy to make a list of things we have lost. Sometimes it is even easier to focus only on what we think we need. But such lists do not inspire solutions. I am not suggesting for one minute that we should sweep the past under the carpet: we need to respect the past but not to let it govern the rest of this precious journey. The reality is that nothing in the past can be changed. It's over. We would all love to return and undo our mistakes. We all carry regrets. But yesterday is over and done with. Other people become obsessed with tomorrow. Will the recession ever end? Is there any point sending children to university? Will they ever have jobs? I am not suggesting that we make ourselves blind to the future; it is often wise to prepare and plan, but so much about tomorrow is not definite. A reality of life is that many people won't wake up tomorrow, but they don't know that today. We must try to not burn too much time on needless worry. Many of our worries are never realised, but we can brew anxiety in our lives and affect the quality of our days by anticipating crises that never happen. We would be in a much better place if we focused more on the gift of today. Often we do not see what's right in front of us: family, friends, reasonably good health, a roof over our heads, food in the fridge, air to breathe. If you lived in Syria, for example, there would be no talk of recession or financial pressure. Millions of people have fled from the country and are living in tents. And Syria is only one place in this world that is experiencing widespread pain and anguish.

I remember being asked to give a presentation on bereavement and grief. It was the first time that I had ever been asked to speak on this topic. The audience would be from my community. I was very conscious that I would be speaking to some very hurt people. Bereavement is a personal journey and the more I prepared my talk, the more nervous I became. My own personal experience of grief stemmed from the loss of both my parents. I could only understand the hurt of loss from my own perspective. I could not assume that anyone else experienced the same pain because we all have different relationships with parents. We can lose them at different stages of our life journey. Not only that but the loss of a partner or child is also a totally different experience. The circumstance of death adds another variable to the experiences, be it old age or suicide, for instance. I became increasingly nervous and hoped for a small attendance.

When I got to the venue I was deeply troubled as there was a full capacity audience. As I took my position I glanced down at faces whom I knew. Giving a talk within your own community is more daunting, because you know the life stories of many in the audience. I noticed Bernard. He had lost his beloved daughter Ciara. Would any of my words 'land' with him or anyone in the room at all? How could I truly understand their pain and offer any help for their anguish and pain? And then there was Jacinta. She lost her son through suicide. I gave it my best but no one knew how nervous I was. My back was wet. I was totally out of my comfort zone. Usually I speak about positive topics like happiness. This night I was facing a room full to the rafters of unhappiness. Afterwards some people came up to me and shook my hand. Jacinta was generous enough to say that she found my talk very helpful. There was a sense of relief that at least I hadn't added to anyone's experience of hurt. Her kind words and many handshakes made me feel comfortable again.

Months later, as I was working on a draft of this very chapter, the doorbell rang. It was Bernard. He came to thank me personally. We chatted over a cup of tea. He had decided to visit to thank me for pointers I gave on the night. Being thanked or affirmed has an uplifting effect on you. In this particular instance it renewed my own confidence to speak on the topic of grief and loss. His visit was more important to me than he will ever realise.

Gratitude is a deep appreciation for what you receive, whether tangible or not. Being grateful means acknowledging the goodness in your life. Often the source of goodness lies outside yourself and practising gratitude allows you to connect better with your world, to see beyond yourself and your individual experiences. It can be expressed for simple things like finding your wallet, finishing early from work or noticing that your teenager has tidied his room. We can also be grateful for bigger things like job security, having a happy marriage or being blessed with lifelong friends. It's a practice consistently associated with greater happiness. By integrating more of it in our everyday reality, we will experience more positive emotions, enjoy better health and manage the inevitable crises of life better.

We will be able to put our worries into better context. We can be grateful for past positive life events and memories, perceive each day as a gift, not to be taken for granted, or anticipate good things happening in our future and allow ourselves to be grateful about such possibilities. Practising gratitude more regularly can potentially enhance the quality of our lives and increase our life satisfaction in a profound way.

Strategies for Integrating more Gratitude into Your Life

Give Someone a Thank You Card or Present

We can take people for granted too easily. It may be a senior staff member who helps you settle into your new job or the teacher who encourages you in your work. Your mother may have a remarkable knack of always being there for you in crisis. Putting into words how grateful you are and posting a card or delivering a present to that person may lift their heart. It heightens your sense of the gift that that person was or is in your life and initiates a cascade of positive emotions.

Taking your Blessings to Bed with You

Just before you fall asleep, look back on the day that you had. Challenge yourself to recall the three best things that happened to you since you woke up that morning and vividly visualise them and how you felt at the time.

Write Down the Five Best Things about Your Life at the Moment

Usually people automatically start listing all the people whom they love but the list will expire quickly with this approach.

Leave family and friends out of this exercise and list things that you are very grateful about your life in general. Focus on them and talk about them to your family and friends.

Cultivate Gratitude for the People You Love
Have a private gratitude chat with yourself about the important people in your life as you communicate with them. As you pass the sauce to your partner, remind yourself how fortunate you are to have someone whom you love so much in your life. As you play with your children, talk to yourself about how they are precious gifts in your life. As you watch your father drive away from your home, take a private moment to rejoice that he is healthy and well.

Keep a Gratitude Journal
This would be a special diary where you would commit to writing down the gifts that you have received during the course of each day. Share this information with your loved ones.

Say a Prayer of Gratitude
If you have a religious faith, say a prayer that specifically rejoices in the gladness of the gifts that you have received this day and in your life in general.

6| savouring

*'Plenty of people miss their share
of happiness, not because they never found it,
but because they didn't stop to enjoy it.'*
—William Feather

We become easily lost in the 'noise' of life and never 'hear' ourselves. People regularly say that they don't have time to think. They find themselves always rushing to the next thing or trying to remember the last thing they forgot to do. We spend so much of our energy trying to achieve goals, but when we achieve them, we set even more. We can become exhausted and stressed with this approach to life. We can become engulfed by all the tasks, objectives and goals. Life seems to fly by and it can seem that we are merely passengers on the journey.

Sometimes I escape from my busy work schedule to the west of Ireland. Summer is my favourite time of year because I stop working for about six weeks. During the rest of the year I work hard and travel far. These weeks are different, and act as a retreat. My adrenaline levels lower. I find myself reading, listening to and playing music, walking and spending quality time with the people I love. They help me become more reflective and in tune with myself. My thoughts run more fluently because I am freer. I have more time for myself. I can hear myself think.

I have had a great affinity with Sligo since teaching there in the 1980s. Sligo has numerous sandy beaches where I regularly walk and connect with its majestic surroundings. Rosses Point is one such beach. The first beach is nearest the car park and for that reason is always more populated. The second beach is longer and tends to be less busy; it's more open there, too. After walking the first stretch, you need work your way down to reach the second beach. I am always acutely aware of the power of the wind. Sometimes I stop and stare out to sea. The waves have a rhythm and power that is constant.

If I keep walking and climb over a hump of rocks at the end of the second beach, I will eventually find myself completely alone. Not many people bother with the third beach. I always take the opportunity if the tide allows. I find a quiet corner and lie flat on my back. I close my eyes and listen attentively to the world around me. Distant cars. Grasses swaying. The high-pitched cries of children from the car park. A warm breeze fans my face. Seagulls glide above and I hear waves batter the sands. In moments like this, I come to realise that I am here. Sometimes we are so busy we forget that we are HERE.

I savour these moments, knowing they are precious. I often wonder whether the locals become accustomed to the beauty around them. I feel that I'd never stop seeing, feeling, smelling and tasting its majesty. I think that when we connect to the world around us, we actually start connecting with ourselves. We often do not see or hear the music of the wonderful world that we inhabit.

Savouring means the capacity to attend to the joys, pleasures, and other positive feelings that we experience in our lives. It is when we relish and focus on something enjoyable or satisfying. It is commonly experienced in relation to food, but positive psychology research studies reveal that there are benefits in learning to savour more than a good meal or drink. It is not about grasping for pleasure or reaching out for the next better thing to come our way. We tend to find it easier to savour special moments like a wedding, concert or holiday. On the other hand we sometimes fail to notice everyday pleasures. I have encountered people who live beside the seaside and fail to take in its majesty. But I have also spoken to people who set out in a deliberate way to bask in the glory of it all. Through their daily walk they savour every moment.

By working harder at learning to savour positive memories, we can cheer ourselves up when we're feeling blue. Studies show that savouring positive events is correlated with a greater sense of well-being, greater happiness, and even better health.

When we visit the health section of the library or bookshop, we encounter an array of books about coping with the negative events of life, from relationship break-ups to illness and death. There are few titles about how to harness the positive experiences of life. There seems to be little interest in learning how to experience the positive aspects of life in a deep and meaningful way – of learning how to capture, savour and sustain the magical moments. It is often presumed that when good things happen, we naturally experience joy, but research indicates that this is not the case.

Social psychologist Fred Bryant has investigated the phenomenon of savouring. He has shown that by learning to tune into these golden moments, we can make our relationships stronger and experience better mental and physical health. By savouring the golden moments of our past, focusing more intently on the magic of what we experience in the 'now' and anticipating or imagining future wonderful experiences, we can positively affect our mood and raise our spirits during challenging times.

I was once invited to address the staff at Glenstal Abbey School on the south west coast of Ireland. This fee-paying secondary school is located on the grounds of a monastery in Murroe, County Limerick. The monastery is on a 500-acre estate with streams, lakes and woodland paths, and beside a castle built in the romantic Norman style. The abbey, dedicated to Saints Joseph and Columba, is home to a community of Benedictine monks. Their prayer and liturgical celebration is combined with managing the school, a farm, and a guest house. The monks assemble in the church four times a day for the Divine Office and Mass. Local people and visitors are welcome to join these rituals.

Over the years, many thousands of people have come to the abbey for some 'time out', to create space to 'think', to seek meaning, to invest in their spirituality and to foster the inner peace that so often eludes us. I had another engagement the next day in the University of Limerick, but chose not to stay in a hotel in the city and decided instead to stay in a guesthouse in the grounds within walking distance of the church and refectory. The welcoming Father Christopher, the former abbot who is in charge of the guesthouse, told me about Vespers, the evening prayers that are held every day in the church. This period of chanting would be followed by dinner in the refectory.

He advised me that guests were welcome to join the monks for dinner but that it would be eaten in silence. Conversation is forbidden and the only voice to be heard is that of one solitary monk reading in the background. The atmosphere was unusual, to say the least. But I felt more focused on my food than normal. I found myself concentrating more on it and came to realise how much we fail to savour the gift of flavour. Everything on my plate came from the soil or the animals around the monastery. Research indicates that a slower, more thoughtful way of eating can help with weight problems. Becoming more aware of what we eat could also potentially steer us towards healthier food choices. My silent dinner in the monastery could be dubbed 'mindful eating'. The practice of mindfulness stems from the Buddhist tradition and is about becoming fully aware of all that is happening around you at the moment. These Christian monks were equally mindful of the gift of food. Such a focused approach to food and its consumption is the opposite of most people's hectic and deadline-driven worlds.

Two mindful-eating experts, Ronna Kabatznick, assistant professor in the psychiatry department in the University of California, and Camille Nghiem-Phu, a Toroto-based naturopathic doctor, have completed interesting work in this area. They emphasise the importance of proper chewing, the timing of meals and recognising feelings of fullness. Many people eat during the day without sufficient awareness of these dimensions to eating. When we eat, the stomach organ releases parts of the food to the small intestine in short spurts. When the small intestine senses food entering, it releases a hormone called cholecystokin (CCK) into the bloodstream. This signals to the stomach to slow down the rate of these short spurts. CCK also signals to the brain that we are full and that we can stop eating. When we gobble our food, not only do we miss out on taste but the small intestine cannot keep up. It is as if the system of digestion trips over itself in the rush; CCK cannot be released into the bloodstream to let us know that we have eaten enough.

By eating more slowly, our digestive system can release the appropriate hormones and enzymes for optimal digestion. We should be more mindful of our eating, and notice the colour, smells, flavours and textures of the food on our plates. This is a habit that can be formed with practice. We are less likely to overeat with such an approach because we will be mindful of feeling full. Concentrating on our eating and focusing our attention on the gift of the food is a good example of savouring.

When I was young, we had to come to the table when called for dinner. There was no microwave and dinner would go cold if we were slow to respond. Nowadays, I wonder how many families even sit at the same table for dinner. Sometimes family members eat meals on their laps as they watch television, or talk on the phone. But do we savour the actual flavours of our food? I remember witnessing a frustrated wife chastising her husband for not knowing what she had cooked. He ate it so quickly before rushing back to work that it had escaped him whether it was chops or salmon. A small but growing body of research suggests that by eating more slowly, or more thoughtfully, we can alleviate gastrointestinal problems. But before we can become more mindful when eating, we need to rid ourselves of distractions such as television and mobile phones.

Walking on a beach while absorbing the beauty of nature, or eating slowly and deliberately, focusing on the flavours, are good examples of savouring moments as they happen. But we can also savour moments and experiences from the past or, in anticipation, savour moments that lie ahead. Fred Bryant maintains that people can savour in three time frames: reminiscing about the past, savouring the present moment, and anticipating the future. People tend to find it easier to savour past positive events. Savouring the present and future is less common.

Bryant is adamant that engaging in all three temporal forms of savouring allows us greater opportunity to find joy in these positive experiences. People who are more capable of savouring within these three domains generally report higher quality of life.

Digital cameras were a great invention but sadly, far too often photographs stay inside them; likewise with the photos taken on mobile phones. We do not focus as much as we used to on happy days from our past that are documented in photographs. Only a few decades ago, most family homes had photograph albums stashed on shelves in the living room, to be regularly pored over again and again.

As a child I remember a visiting uncle bringing his projector and collection of slides to our home. Curtains were tightly drawn as we marvelled at the radiant images on the wall. Enthusiastic discussion ensued about who built certain sand-castles, the car my father drove at that time, fashions of the 1970s and how young everyone looked.

Part of life's reality is its imperfection. But we can savour the good times by vividly recalling them or by sharing the memories with others. Recalling golden days from our lives re-energises us into the future and cultivates a sense of gratitude, which serves us well. By working harder at learning to savour positive memories, we can cheer ourselves up when we're feeling blue.

Photographs or video clips are one way of reinforcing positive and uplifting memories. We can also store mental images and return to them to help us focus more clearly on the event and reap the positive feelings of those moments. I met a woman who told me that she sends herself to sleep every night by recalling the happy times in her life. Adding prayer to these positive reflections also helps her sleep better, she maintained.

And who could argue with that? It's better to fall asleep vividly savouring what went well that day rather than reliving its anxious or stressed moments.

An interesting study by Jordi Quoidbach and colleagues in 2010 indicates that wealth may impair our ability to savour positive emotions and experiences. In a sample of working adults, wealthier individuals reported a lower savouring ability. The negative impact of wealth on participants in the study undermined the positive effects of money on their happiness. Wealth may actually fail to deliver the happiness expected of it, because it is detrimental to our ability to savour. Maybe this is down to the fact that the more we have, the less we tend to savour.

Sometimes we completely fail to notice the good things that happen. When receiving praise for efforts at work or celebrating winning a prize in a draw, some people don't let these events sink in properly. They move on swiftly. Or worse still, sometimes we make little of these events. We attribute the praise to a lenient boss or explain our luck in the draw as the result of a low number of entries. A compliment can be interpreted cynically or embraced in its entirety.

Bryant maintains that we have a habitual predisposition to savour or not. He has shown that it is a stable characteristic that can be reliably measured through surveys ascertaining how frequently people derive pleasure from strategies such as anticipating pleasurable events and relishing them in the moment. His research has shown that people who habitually savour are happier and more satisfied with life in general, more optimistic and less depressed than those who do not savour.

Bryant and Joseph Veroff conducted extensive research into savouring. In 2006 they identified it as a theoretical model for conceptualising and understanding the psychology of enjoyment. They understood savouring as a process through which people manage positive emotions. In their opinion it most vividly captured the active process of enjoyment, the ongoing interplay between a person and their environment. They differentiate between pleasure and savouring, even though these are intimately connected concepts: when we savour something, we are aware of pleasure and appreciate the positive feelings experienced. In their opinion, however, we don't necessarily savour simply by experiencing pleasure. In order to savour, we must be attentive and have an appreciative awareness of the pleasure.

For Bryant and Veroff, savouring is a mindful state. Although, more often than not, savouring can come from unplanned, impromptu moments, there are mechanisms in which the cognitive and behavioural processes of it can be invoked to set up conducive conditions for savouring to occur in the future, processes based on what people are going through psychologically when they actively savour in the present.

Bernie's three sons emigrated to Australia. Two of them are married with their own families and the younger son recently became engaged. Their father died before they left Ireland. Although she admits to periods of immense loneliness, she has hundreds of photographs carefully compiled into categorised chapters and themes. On a recent visit she brought me on a detailed tour of memories and events from her family's history using these photographs. 'I may be lonely now,' she said, 'but we had great times and I love remembering them.' She added that she can almost place herself back in those photographs and relive the moment they were taken.

For her the photos are not merely relics of her past. They are not instruments for fostering loneliness or regret. Rather, she returns to the preciousness of these moments and savours them. Many people become engulfed by their work. I often advise such people to plan a special day in the future dedicated to savouring. It's not that I want them to restrict savouring to a few days a year – the more we savour, the happier we feel – but what I am suggesting is that they legislate for periods of more intense savouring. Savouring may be enhanced if we travel to a beautiful place on our own. In our own company, we are removed from the stresses and strains of everyday life. We can concentrate on the world around us in a focused and deliberate way. We could take a digital camera and capture some of the sights on the way back. Later that evening we could revisit the scene through the photographs we had taken and conjure up the same emotions that we felt earlier that day. Other people may feel that using a camera would disrupt the process. If that is the case they could take some 'mental photographs' to revisit later.

Sometimes we may feel like writing about a special day. I often attempt to capture moments when I savour the beauty around me through writing about it. I found this example in one of my journals. I wrote these lines after a sudden and heavy snowfall and can read them at any time to bring me back to its beauty:

> The snow covers all the bumps and loose stones on the avenue. It slides its cloak over the brazen blades of neglected grasses. It smothers the water in the tin buckets and dresses the trees in white wedding gowns. It throws its sheet over the top of the drumlins as a signal for all to fall asleep deeply. Nature's world has been called into hiding. We have been blindfolded

of the tapestry of everyday November colours. We should savour the might and glory of the White Princess but remind ourselves of the miracle of the everyday reality that we sometimes fail to see around us.

The following strategies based on Bryant's work can enhance our ability to savour. These are some that work best for me.

How to Savour More

Share Your Positive Feelings with Others

When we receive good news, our first instinct is nearly always to tell someone. Bryant recommends that we approach positive events in the same way. We should tell others when we are feeling particularly appreciative of a certain event or moment. For example, if we are enjoying a meal with family and friends, we should formally articulate to them that we are appreciating it. Studies about the way people react to positive events show that those who share their positive experiences with others are happier overall than those who do not.

Compile a Library of Mental Photographs

An example of this is where you would consciously make yourself deeply aware of something you want to remember later. You may be standing on the beach and decide to concentrate your mind on the red hue around the clouds or the gliding seagulls in the distance. There may be one mountain higher than others. You log this picture in your mind and try to see it again in your memory later that night.

Congratulate Yourself

Sometimes we wake up dreading the difficult day ahead but when we successfully come through such days, we need to affirm ourselves. People who revel in the successes have been shown to enjoy the outcome better than those who don't. It's not about massaging your ego but about acknowledging that something good happened and focusing on this rather than taking our customary dismissive attitude towards the positive.

Maximise Your Senses

Aim to utilise your sensory perception more. Taste your food, feel the texture of a leaf, smell the roses, see the colours in the sky and listen out for the cello in the orchestra. Concentrate and allow yourself to become immersed. I remember growing a small 'garden' of herbs in pots along the kitchen window. My children had great fun guessing the flavours as they tasted the leaves. Coriander, mint and rosemary are examples of truly wonderful flavours straight from the soil. So many children grow up without even knowing where flavours come from.

I know a man with a CD collection that fills an entire room. He treats himself to Mozart's *Requiem* as often as he can. He says he finds the piece therapeutic. He tells me that it moves him at a very deep level every time he plays it. I know another man who visits art galleries wherever he travels. He is not an artist himself but becomes immersed in these galleries. They are like windows to someone's life or forgotten times and he savours the intrinsic skills used by each artist in every painting he examines. Running your hand along a sculpture (if allowed!) or through the veins of a leaf can help connect you more deeply. The wine connoisseur can sense flavours in the wine that cannot be explained in terms of content. But these flavours are deemed unique to a particular bottle and savoured accordingly.

Celebrate Your Successes

When you pass your driving test, succeed in cooking a complex recipe, win a prize, are called for an interview, or lose weight – celebrate these moments in a very deliberate way. See them as opportunities to rejoice in life, no matter how small they seem. Make them big in your own eyes. People who express their emotions at these times enjoy them so much more. Life will always pose challenges and these will sap our energy. We seem to find it easier to concentrate on the negative events, but we should form a habit of savouring our success.

Compare the Negative Outcome to Something Worse

If we burned the stew, remember those who have no food. If we failed a maths exam, discuss the subjects that you didn't fail. If you struggle with your job, remind yourself of how fortunate you are to have a job. This helps us bounce out of the negative event and keeps things in perspective. It's not that we deny the negative, rather we protect ourselves from becoming engulfed by it. Contextualising by reminding ourselves of worst-case scenarios can help us deal with negative events.

Remind Ourselves that Time Passes

Yesterday is gone. Tomorrow has still to come. Our good moments don't last forever and that's why we need to cherish them more. Realising how short-lived certain moments can be helps us enjoy them while they happen.

Benedict was telling me that he lives for his two gorgeous daughters, aged seven and five. He was saying all the right things, but I startled him when I asked if he ever had time to bring them to the playground. Children grow up quickly and I have met parents who regret not having the time to grow with them. I didn't mean to unsettle him but I am conscious of the fact that we can know the right things to do, but can still fail to do them.

By reminding ourselves that our loved ones are precious gifts in our lives we may connect with them in a more meaningful way. Often we are too stressed or busy to play with our children. But time passes by quickly and the truth is that they will not always be children. Likewise with an elderly parent, sick brother or sister or distant friend. It's important to cherish the key people in our lives through the various chapters of our life story.

7| spirituality and prayer

*'The foundations of a person
are not in matter but in spirit.'*
—Ralph Waldo Emerson

The parked trolleys lining the corridor made it difficult for other traffic to pass. Visitors stepped into the wards to allow trolleys by as nurses scrambled to keep drips and charts intact. It was a highly stressed environment. Agitated patients queued for attention. The under-resourced staff was barely coping with the pressures of their overburdened schedules. I had visited many hospitals in a personal or professional capacity but this was different. This time I was lying flat on a parked trolley, waiting to see a specialist. Detached from family and friends, I waited and waited. The pain in my side was unbearable and my anxiety was further exacerbated by what seemed an eternal delay.

Although medication eventually numbed the pain, I was still on the trolley that night, with eight other patients of different gender, age and backgrounds. Diagnosed with appendicitis, I was on the list for surgery in the morning. An elderly lady on the trolley in front of me sporadically whispered her prayers.

The man behind coughed and spluttered and ensured broken sleep for everyone most of the night. During the early hours, nurses did their best to command a silence but conversations inevitably became louder as patients asked questions.

My night was punctuated with pensive thoughts: my mobile was dead and I had no connection with the people I loved most. Maybe it was this prolonged period of solitude, my sense of detachment, or the fact that I was totally unaccustomed to being a patient in hospital, but I started to think intensely about my health (or ill-health). I hoped that the experts were correct with their diagnosis. Worry set in.

Sometimes people die in hospitals. Sometimes unexpected complications arise. Imagine if the course of my life was about to change dramatically. Imagine if this was my last night on earth. This body, this mind, this personality, this mystery that is 'I', would cease to be. My life worries faded as I contemplated this idea. A deep loneliness and remoteness engulfed me. My dreams might never be realised. I might never witness my children's graduations or weddings, or hold their children in my arms.

I questioned even more deeply – is this it? When this biological representation of me ceases to have life within it – is that it? Will there be another dimension to me? Will this consciousness that defines me and my world cease to exist? Will it take another form? Will there be a new experience or a new consciousness? Will it remember or connect with this one? Is there a God? Another world after this?

Almost without thinking, I started to pray. The fact that I resorted to prayer was related to my religious upbringing. My parents had a deep faith and we'd always prayed together as a family, especially when I was young. In this unsettled frame of mind, I turned spontaneously to prayer. And my prayers calmed me as I fell asleep.

As a child, I remember my sense of insecurity in the dark when the moon played tricks with creases in curtains, or when my heightened sensitivity allowed fear to amplify the ordinary sounds of night. I often said a prayer or two and fell asleep. The prayers seemed to ease my fears. As an adult, my prayers are more infrequent and my faith far more precarious than that of an unquestioning child. However, I have encountered many people with a profound belief in God and a deep commitment to regular prayer. Scientific studies have established that there may be psychological and physiological benefits in prayer.

There are people reading these lines who would never have troubled moments such as I had that night. They would maintain that they never contemplate such thoughts about existence and the meaning of life, that even if they were awaiting test results in the doctor's surgery or gravely ill in a hospital bed, they would not turn their minds to a god. They see prayer, religion and faith as useless possessions in a search for meaning that cannot be found. They would be adamant that there is nothing to believe in.

Maybe such people have abandoned religion or faith because their maturing scientific minds have dismissed it as time-wasting, a total nonsense. Maybe they never believed in anything and don't care. But the quest for meaning and personal beliefs around such matters can be relevant in the context of living life well. Religious practices have been shown to foster health, resilience and a sense of inner peace.

The prayers I said that night brought me calmness. In my case there was a spiritual and not merely a psychological or physiological dimension to this, as I personally believe in God and an afterlife. My prayers that night were a form of communication with a divine being. Not everybody reading this book will have a similar belief system. But that is not what is at issue here. The question is whether it was my prayers that gave me a sense of calm in that moment.

It's important to acknowledge that religion has contributed to war and destruction and can foster harmful, negative emotions and influences. It is at the heart of many of the world's bloodstained trouble spots. Religion can be over-controlling and stunt human beings' ability to think for themselves. It can prevent people from accommodating or tolerating other religious viewpoints, or those with none, but there is growing research indicating that religion is not all bad. Practices encouraged within religion, the social connectedness associated with the rituals or gatherings, the sense of spirituality encapsulated through prayer, the sense of purpose or meaning offered by theology and the love and compassion promoted through doctrine, can have positive effects on our moods and approach to life. This chapter can only touch on the topic. Religion and spirituality are very personal phenomena and seem to be intertwined, particularly when people start talking about one, the other, or both.

Spirituality or Religiousness?

Spirituality and religion are receiving increased attention from scientists because of their possible link to mental health promotion and the prevention of mental illness. Although findings are somewhat equivocal, indications are that religious practice, affiliation and belief are beneficial for mental health. Studies of both will always prove problematic because scientists as well as practitioners of faith have failed to differentiate between them. Another complication is that some people can be spiritual and not religious. Likewise, people may practise religion and not claim to be particularly spiritual. Religions come in many shapes and sizes with different values, morals, rules and regulations, and can be based within varied cultures. Spirituality is broader and much harder than religion to define and measure and, as a consequence, there are more studies into the benefits of religious practice. It is somewhat easier to explore aspects of religious involvement and beliefs that may influence health outcomes. As a result there has been a significant growth in studies that are more robust, which provide evidence that suggest religious involvement and practice is associated with better physical and mental health and a longer life. Such studies have not provided sufficient clarity on the mechanisms involved, however. Scientist Linda K. George argues that scientific scrutiny in this area cannot be complete without a comprehensive understanding of these mechanisms. We would also need to identify the active ingredients before they could ever be promoted as contributory factors to health and well-being. Perhaps the active ingredients can be cultivated outside religious constraints and with comparable benefit.

The Phenomenon of Prayer

Prayer is not something people talk about openly except with their peers in a prayer group or when availing of spiritual guidance. In modern society we tend to look suspiciously on anyone who speaks often or too publicly about their personal prayer life. The fall from grace and influence of the institution-alised church has made it nearly politically inappropriate to wear your religion, if you still have one, on your sleeve. In a society that celebrates scientific and technological gains, prayer is sometimes regarded as something with no science behind it, and merely a ritual practised by innocent or misguided people.

There has been a growth in research into prayer in recent decades. Earlier studies were based on very small samples and were fundamentally flawed. They tended to be in the form of anecdotal reports of miracles. However, more systematic inves-tigations and increased clinical research has been conducted in the last ten years. Professional bodies have issued position papers in support of this research and more funding has been made available for it. In nearly all religions, prayer is the most ubiquitous and personal of religious experiences. It is a critical and central practice to each religion and the religious experi-ence. It is also profoundly spiritual as it represents mediation between a person and who they perceive as a supreme being – a connection to the sacred. Prayer is also deeply meditative and may therefore convey many of the health benefits that have been confirmed to be associated with meditation in general.

Harvard scientist Herbert Benson has focused almost exclusively on meditation from the Buddhist tradition but maintains that all forms of deep prayer evoke a relaxation response that alleviates stress and calms the body. Often prayer involves repetition of sounds or words. For Catholics, it may be the Rosary, for Jews it's called davening and for monks it is chanting. According to MRI scans, physical changes can be observed in brains during meditation. As an individual goes deeper and deeper into concentrated mediation, intense activity takes place in the parietal lobe circuits. These control a person's orientation in space and establish distinctions between the self and the world. Benson has documented what he calls a 'quietude' where the brain becomes enveloped in calmness. The frontal and temporal lobe circuits, which map time and create self-awareness, become disengaged. It's as if one transfers into a heightened emotional state and experiences a sense of awe in the present moment.

Research has also shown that the thickening of the brain cortex associated with regular meditation or other religious or spiritual practice may protect against developing depression. Professor Lisa Miller, director of clinical psychology at Columbia University, has shown this to apply particularly in people predisposed to depression. Her study focused on 103 adults at either high or low risk of depression based on family history. Those subjects who placed a high value on religion or spirituality were shown to have thicker cortices compared to those who did not. Thicker cortices indicate a smaller chance of developing depression. More research is needed to make the case more compelling, but her findings suggest that spirituality or religion may protect against major depression. Meditation has been found to produce a clinically significant reduction in resting as well as ambulatory blood pressure, as well as reducing heart rate, altering levels of melatonin and serotonin, boosting the immune system, reducing stress, and improving mood. Many religions incorporate various forms of meditative practice within them.

Psychologist John Maltby and colleagues from Sheffield Hallam University conducted a prayer study involving 251 men and 223 women between the ages of 18 and 29. They measured participants' reasons for their religious belief, church attendance and tendency to depression. In relation to both men and women, they found that the frequency with which they prayed was closely correlated with having fewer symptoms of depression and anxiety. They also found that those who incorporated prayer into their lives not only were less likely to be mentally ill, but enjoyed higher self-esteem.

Scientific research on the health benefits of prayer is still in its infancy. In order to truly understand why people derive health benefits from prayer, researchers need to identify the unique markers that differentiate prayer from other non-spiritual practices. This is the greatest challenge for science in this area of research. There may be dimensions to prayer that go beyond the reach of science. For an array of reasons, research on the healing or calming benefits of prayer is complicated with assumptions, challenges and contradictions. It is a problematic area for science as there are so many different forms of it: for example, contemplative-meditative, ritual, petitionary, colloquial (adoration) and intercessory. All this makes the area of research complex and practically a minefield for scientists. It could also be argued that the benefits associated with prayer are largely due to repeating mantras and possibly the meditative effects that follow, but many people with a deep religious faith would take a different perspective.

Religion and Coping with Grief

I remember meeting Kathleen. I had just made a presentation to a group of business people in the south west of Ireland and as I was packing my laptop away she approached and asked, 'Can I speak to you for a minute?' I am used to the fact that there will always be a couple of people who want to talk about personal matters when I finish my presentations. I never have enough time for these people, particularly at the end of a long day, but I would never turn my back on them. After listening briefly, I can usually point them to the support service or professional that they need.

I thought Kathleen was another person like this. She started by telling me that her husband had died in his sleep a year ago. I sympathised and she continued, 'And my only son was killed in a car accident six months later.' I was deeply moved and determined to give this heartbroken woman my attention despite my tiredness. But she wasn't there to seek my advice. She had sat through my presentation on the topic of resilience and found my strategies for staying mentally strong in crisis most helpful.

'But you left one thing out of your talk,' she said.

'What?' I asked.

'Prayer,' she replied. 'Prayer has kept me sane.'

I sat down with her then for about 30 minutes. She was still hurting and her life would never be the same, but her faith had carried her through, she said. She leaned on it to keep herself together when her world was falling apart. Kathleen said that at times she felt the presence of her late husband and son. She believed that they were still with her and that she would meet them again. She prayed for them and prayed to them. A profound and deep belief system underpinned her prayers: words were not merely a mantra to keep her healthy but a form of communication with God and indeed with her husband and son.

Whatever you may think of such a belief system, there is no denying that it is a source of strength to Kathleen. I have encountered hundreds of people who are adamant that their faith helped them through dark periods. They further explain their belief that life does not end with death. These beliefs give their lives meaning. It may not be a specific faith, the actual words prayed, or whom is prayed to, but this religiousness or spirituality helps people. There is scientific evidence that spiritual beliefs, like those expressed by Kathleen, may affect the outcome of bereavement.

There is some evidence to suggest that belief in an afterlife allows an acceptance of death and helps facilitate the resolution of grief. In a 2002 study by Walsh and colleagues, 135 relatives and close friends of those who died at a palliative care centre were examined nine months and fourteen months after a bereavement. Using standardised measures of grief, people with no spiritual beliefs did not resolve their grief over the period of the experiment. By contrast, those with strong beliefs resolved their grief progressively over the same period. Participants with low levels of belief were slower to resolve their grief, but did eventually make progress. This would suggest that faith can carry people through dark periods in their lives.

Religious Practice and Happiness

Professor Andrew Clark and Dr Orsolya Lelkes, based at the Paris School of Economics, conducted a study in 2009 into the possible link between religion and happiness. Using data from a representative sample of nearly 30,000 people from 22 European countries, they found that religious people had greater 'life satisfaction' than non-religious people, and this remained consistent even when variables such as age, employment status and marital status were controlled. Prayer and churchgoing were shown to have a statistically significant positive impact on life satisfaction, with churchgoing having a more positive impact than prayer. Their research also showed that challenging life crises had a less negative impact on churchgoers and those who prayed, in comparison with the non-religious group.

Religious beliefs and practice were shown to influence happiness in a report by Paul Dolan, professor of economics at Tanaka Business School, Imperial College London. The 2006 report, which was aimed at helping formulate policy for the British government, showed that the effect was not restricted to any particular religion but that religious beliefs and practices seemed to influence the impact of low income on happiness rates.

Religion and Health: Is There a Connection?

Harold Koenig, MD, associate professor of medicine and psychiatry at Duke University School of Medicine, has studied religious beliefs and their effects on personal health. As senior author of the *Handbook of Religious Health* he tooth-combed through 1200 studies on the effects of prayer on health, and concluded that religious people tend to live healthier lives. Hundreds of studies confirm a positive correlation between religious practice and improved health outcomes. Religion tends to promote a general lifestyle that fosters a better quality of life.

If we take Christianity as an example, its teachings urge Christians to care for their neighbours, forgive their enemies, be grateful, turn away from violence, help the poor, be generous of heart, respect life and the body, honour parents and the elderly, and use their talents. Religions and their 'rules for living' are factors, when applied, to achieving better health outcomes. For example, some religions have very particular rules about diet and alcohol use. Religions often discourage self-indulgence or overindulgence and promote a sense of moderation. The health benefits of religion suggested in these studies relate to the fact that those who practise religion are more likely to engage in habits that promote or enhance health.

Researchers from the University of Michigan analysed data from an annual survey of high school seniors from 135 schools in 48 states in a study called *Monitoring the Future* (Wallace and Forman, 1998). Their findings showed that religious involvement had a large impact on the lifestyles of these students, especially in late adolescence. Students who maintained that religion was important in their lives and attended religious services frequently had lower rates of cigarette smoking, alcohol use, and marijuana use, high rates of seatbelt use, and of eating fruits, vegetables and breakfast. They were also found to be less likely to carry weapons, get into fights or drive while drinking. In a study by Robert Hummer and colleagues at the University of Texas at Austin, life expectancy for individuals at age 20 who attended religious practice regularly was, on average, seven-and-a-half years longer than those who never or rarely attended. The effect proved to be even stronger for African Americans, who showed nearly double the average for Caucasian participants in the study.

In 2000, a meta-analysis by McCullough and colleagues of 42 independent samples, representing 125,826 adults, found that weekly or greater religious service attendance yielded 29 per cent fewer deaths than did nonattendance. In 2003, similar work by Linda Powell and colleagues examined the association between religion, health and life expectancy and confirmed a strong, consistent reduction in mortality rates being present in religious populations who specifically engaged in regular religious attendance. In 2001, Koenig reviewed 52 published cross-sectional studies investigating the religion–longevity association and found evidence of longer survival for those who reported greater religiousness.

Religion and Social Connectivity

One explanation often offered in the relationship of religiousness to health is the social support that is fostered by belonging to a religious community. Being a member of a social group also means that you are more likely to support and be supported. A study from Duke University found that regular attendees at religious services reported larger social networks overall, more frequent telephone and in-person contact, and a stronger feeling of support from their social circles. Religious congregations are often unique as social institutions in that their membership includes the old and the very young. Religious social support is effective because religious congregations provide an environment where people with similar values, interests and activities meet regularly. Often a high degree of emotional care through companionship and prayer support is provided through them. Christopher Ellison and colleagues also reported in 1994 that frequent religious participation was not only related to an increased number of social ties and interactions compared to non-religious individuals, but also to greater appreciation for those same ties. Public religiousness (regular attendance, perceived religious social support) is more strongly associated to health outcomes than private forms of religiousness (frequency of personal prayer, self-regulated religiousness).

The Catholic Church was the dominant church in Ireland for many decades and practically the whole community of a town or village gathered together for Mass each Sunday. Most now acknowledge that the Church had too much power and influence. Our political system reflected its values and our constitution interwove its rules and regulations into our political and legal system. Due to numerous sexual-abuse scandals, coupled with a powerful push towards a secular society, the same Church is in a weakened position today. Its state of decline is reflected in the depleting church attendances.

But the reality is that the churches and chapels also acted as hubs of social connectivity for a nation. When I was young we prayed at Mass for the sick, the new born and the dead. We connected with our community. Our experiences at these religious gatherings elevated us from our narrow selves and helped us see our lives and the world from a different perspective – a worldview. There was a sense of belonging that possibly had much greater psychological implications that we realised at the time. I am not suggesting that we need to go back to the days when churches were full, or when the Catholic Church was in charge. But we may have lost more than we realise by rejecting religion.

Leaning on Religion during Challenging Times

Religious practice also may help people meet challenges and may contribute to a sense of journey and of the future, and foster a sense of purpose or meaning in people's lives. Prayer – because of the belief systems that underpin it – can harness hope. If you face a serious illness, a belief that God is protecting you could potentially strengthen your resolve. Praying to God may alleviate your worries about money, your children or your future because you place it all in God's hands. It could be that meaning derived from religious beliefs and practices is an important mechanism that helps people cope better and achieve better mental health outcomes. Koenig and Larson (2001) have suggested that meaning provides a sense of purpose and direction. How individuals frame their worldview in a religious context can potentially have profound implications for their mental, emotional and physical life.

I remember speaking to Eamonn, who was undergoing treatment for cancer. I asked him if he prayed. He replied, 'Not until now. I'm praying hard now to help me through this.' In his crisis he turned to prayer but had little or no religious practice before his diagnosis. He told me that his new faith was helping him cope. I remember my mother asking for the hospital chaplain and requesting Communion. She held the Divine Mercy prayer card in her hand. The week before she died, when we knew her death was near, I noticed it had fallen on the ground. I remember thinking 'A lot of good that was,' as I picked it up and put it back on her locker. It wasn't until years later that I considered that her prayers probably helped her more than I would ever know. I can also vividly recall my father nursing his rosary beads when he faced terminal illness.

Believers may refer to their suffering as something that will earn them greater rewards in the next life. They sometimes allow their suffering to focus on others who also suffer, maybe more than they suffer themselves. Christians will always recall the suffering of Christ. Renowned psychiatrist Patricia Casey refers to a 'cognitive appraisal' that sets in, where their beliefs allow them to make better sense of their plight and move forward rather than surrender.

Religiousness may influence the course and outcome of illnesses. Harris *et al.* (1995) also showed religion to be associated with better recovery from physical illness, including better health and longer survival after heart transplant and reduced mortality following other cardiac surgeries (Oxman, Freeman and Manheimer, 1995). It also correlated to reduced mortality among breast cancer patients (Spiegel *et al.*, 1989). In a review of over 200 studies examining the relationship between religious commitment and physical health problems including cardiovascular disease, hypertension and stroke, it was shown that religion exerted a positive effect regardless of the outcomes or diseases examined (Levin and Schiller, 1987). In a review (Levin and Vanderpool, 1987) of 27 published cross-sectional studies that investigated the relationship between overall physical health and religious service attendance, similar results were found. Religious service attendance in church, synagogue or mosque was positively associated with overall health status.

What gives our lives meaning? Positive psychology pioneer Martin Seligman advocates that it is through using our 'signature strengths' and virtues in the service of something much larger than we are. In his research, the search for a meaningful life involves seeking a happiness that is distinct from pursuing pleasurable experiences or optimal engagement. This does not mean that we need to exclude pleasurable or flow experiences to achieve more meaning in our lives. But possibly we need to look beyond ourselves and our immediate needs or comforts to feel that our lives have a sense of purpose. It seems we need pleasure but also meaning in our life to feel truly satisfied. Many people seek another *dimension* and look to God. By tapping into a set of religious beliefs, practices and prayer, they may be reaping benefits that they are not fully aware of or that science can fully explain.

8| bouncibility

'It is not the strongest of the species
that survive, nor the most intelligent,
but the one most responsive to change.'
—Charles Darwin

have addressed many groups throughout Ireland, including teachers, health-care professionals, business people and community groups. The topic varies depending on the needs of the specific group in question, but I am always conscious of one reality that binds everyone in the audience and me together – the reality that we all face challenges and crises. This world is a wonderful place, but it is an imperfect journey dotted with unpleasant experiences. We do not have full control over our destiny. Our genetics play a significant role in the quality of our lives and length of time that we will live. You are growing older even as you read this book and will inevitably look older too (although hopefully not as a consequence of reading it). We have no say in this reality.

Another reality is that we will all die. And family members and friends will die, too. Science cannot turn either of these realities on their heads. Ever since we were born, things happened that we did not want to experience. Sadly, we are not prepared for these realities: we are never taught how to cope during challenging times. The educational system fails to unearth our potential not only to survive but to thrive during the inevitable crises of life. We tend to assume that children learn these skills through their experiences; that having learned the requisite academic skills, they are ready for life. The truth is that even successful academic achievement does not necessarily allow children to become self-reliant citizens who will realise their true potential.

When we start school we are confronted by an abundance of unfamiliar faces and personalities for the first time. After many years' adaptation to the system of having one teacher for the whole school year, this new experience is one of encountering numerous teachers during the course of a single day. More bells have to be followed, an unfamiliar environment needs to be adjusted to, new subjects need to be accustomed to and classrooms packed with strange faces can be a daunting experience, to say the least.

You may have been one of the many children that cried when left in the hands of a teacher on that historic first day. It may have been your first time waving a reluctant goodbye to your mother, father or guardian. Your instinct told you that this parting would be for a long time. It was something you didn't want to happen, but you had no control over it. Within days you may have encountered, for the first time, someone who disliked you for no good reason. Maybe another child was mean or unfriendly. You could no longer run into the arms of your parent for comfort. School was also the first time in your life when your literacy and numeracy abilities were uncovered. It became even more upsetting when you noted how some other children seemed to find the task easier than you did. The beaming pride of your parent was replaced by the disappointed frown of your teacher.

Over time, you and most of your peers adapted to the new experiences of school life. You became familiar with your surroundings, made new friends and became accustomed to the teacher's raised voice. Many children grow to love school. Most of us have this same capacity to adapt to new experiences. However, some people become stuck or regress in the midst of challenge. The reality of life is that it can present us with more daunting and wounding experiences than settling into school. We can encounter experiences that have the potential to knock us down for life.

How do people deal with the difficult events that change their lives? The death of a loved one, the loss of a job or serious illness, or traumatic events such as terrorist attacks or tsunamis: these are examples of trying events that can potentially ruin the remaining days of our lives. Such events propel us into an unaccustomed domain of insecurity and uncertainty. They can induce the deepest emotions and leave a permanent mark. We can become engulfed and lose the will to live. I have met people who collapsed under the shadow of crisis and never really recovered their zest for life. They became mere passengers on the journey. I have met others who possessed an ability to weather the storms, to keep health and hurt in the same room, to tap into their resources and reclaim their right to have the best possible life despite what has happened.

This innate ability to adapt in the face of adversity, trauma, tragic loss, profound disappointment, injustice or other significant sources of stress such as serious health problems, financial or workplace upheaval, is called resilience. If crises are part and parcel of life, it seems a grave pity that we do not intervene at an early stage to arm our children with the coping skills and buffers to protect them. The growing research in resilience is exciting in that by learning from the survivors or the people who 'bounce back' from crisis, we can potentially teach these critical skills or legislate for the necessary buffers.

According to psychologist and resilience expert Ann Masten, resilience is not acquired through some rare or extraordinary process but through ensuring that some basic human adaptive systems are operating normally. She maintains that children and adults have an impressive capacity to be resilient when basic protections are in place and working. Levels of resilience are built when children experience an environment in which they feel protected and encouraged, and enjoy the emotional security of close relationships (human or spiritual) when their brains are functioning normally for learning, problem-solving and trouble-shooting, when they experience hope and self-empowerment. She maintains that the greatest threats to human resilience are circumstances that damage or destroy these basic protections.

For example, if a child loses his caregiver, it's critical that care and functional parenting is still provided. Science is continuing to learn about our fundamental protective systems and the implications of promoting resilience in individuals, families and communities, both before and after adversity. Science is also interested in what it terms 'risk factors'. A risk factor is usually defined as something that increases the likelihood of a future negative outcome for a child (Durlak, 1998), while a 'protective factor' is a variable that decreases such a probability. In essence, protective factors can be broadly grouped into four domains – child, family, school and community.

A more detailed analysis of the psychology of resilience and related studies would be best served in a book dedicated to those areas. For the purposes of this book, I want to examine protective factors or traits to help readers integrate them into their lives.

Noel was a highly skilled entrepreneur who built up his own property-management company during the Celtic Tiger years. He had invested his profits prudently and had a strong portfolio but, within a space of six months, he was wiped out and was bankrupt by the end of 2010. His best friend Barry had taken the same career path and became a wealthy man. His livelihood was also destroyed following the economic collapse.

Both men went into a downward spiral, experiencing profound anxiety, a deep sense of failure, insomnia and an intense sense of hopelessness. Noel described it as sliding down an oiled rope: no grip and an inevitable thump to the ground. For him, the cloud of doom lifted after approximately eight months. He concluded that his downfall was not entirely his own doing. The economy had collapsed – but that was not his fault, it was a worldwide phenomenon. He was also acutely aware of many others who had been similarly affected. He knew of people who had lost their marriages, and even some very sad cases of suicide. By the end of his bankruptcy process, he was already planning his comeback, had accessed money for new business ideas and formed new strategic partnerships. He also did something he hadn't done for twenty years – work for someone else.

Barry had moved from a deep sadness to a profound depression. He was also suffering severe anxiety and was unable to contemplate a return to any type of work. According to Barry, he had failed himself, his family and his community. He would never risk bringing such failure upon himself again.

The reality is that there are many Noels and Barrys out there. They can be contrasted in how they make sense of failure;

in fact, they are polar opposites in this. You and I know that it is the Noels of this world who truly succeed in business while people like Barry eventually find themselves cornered or 'stuck'. But is it possible to differentiate between the Barrys and the Noels? It's clear that Noel is blessed with resilience. Is it possible to train Barry to be more resilient?

Martin Seligman is famous for his investigative work into positive traits in humans but did not begin in this area. His initial research in the 1960s was on failure and helplessness: with colleagues he first discovered 'learned helplessness'. Through experimental work, they learned that dogs, rats, mice and even cockroaches that experienced mildly painful shock, over which they had no control, would eventually succumb to it. They accepted it and made no attempt to escape.

In 1975, Seligman and researcher Donald Hiroto showed that human beings do the same. Subjects were randomly divided into three groups. The first group was subjected to loud noise that participants could stop by pushing a button in front of them. The second group was subjected to the same loud noise but had no way of switching it off. The third group, the control group, was not subjected to any noise. The following day, the subjects faced a new scenario. To turn the noise off, all they had to do was move their hands approximately twelve inches. The people in the first and third groups figured this out and readily learned how to turn the noise off.

Subjects in the second group typically did nothing. In the first phase of the experiment, they had tried and failed to switch off the noise. They learned that they had no control and became passive and effortless: in essence, they had learned to be helpless. The second phase of the experiment demonstrated learned helplessness because this group expecting failure failed to try.

Seligman believes that the critical factor differentiating Noel from Barry may be optimism. His studies of humans and animals that experience inescapable shock or noise indicate that approximately one-third never become helpless. Through comprehensive surveying, Seligman and colleagues analysed the content of verbatim speech and writing of subjects to examine how they explain their failures. Their explanatory style, being either optimistic or pessimistic, was key. The people who had a tendency not to give up interpreted their setbacks as temporary, local and changeable. In other words, they believed that the setback was not permanent, was merely one difficult but specific situation, and that something could be done about it. The people who became helpless interpreted the setback as permanent. It was not seen as one specific failure but an indication of failure in life as a whole. They also had a tendency to personalise it and blame it on themselves.

Pessimism is not all bad, while optimism for the sake of it is foolhardy. But we all need to have at least the ability to countenance optimism. Seligman has shown that it is possible to identify people with a negative or pessimistic bias. With innovative programmes at schools in the US, he and his colleagues have shown that optimism can be taught to beneficial effect. A little bit of optimism can make a big difference in a crisis and we need it among our repertoire of responses.

Dr Karen Reivich and Andrew Shatte have dedicated many years to researching the area of resilience. Reivich initially believed that people were either born resilient or not. However, resilience is not all or nothing. People vary in resilience and can be resilient in some situations but not in others. The good news is that we can all learn to be more resilient. We can learn from crisis and build our resilience for any future crises that may ensue. Reivich and Shatte have identified seven areas where resilient people tend to be strong. We can all work on these strengths and become more resilient. I have been privileged to meet many survivors of crisis who reclaim their right to have the best possible life despite severe setbacks and disappointment. I have found threads of what Reivich has identified as resilient traits in the stories of such people. The seven key traits that Reivich has highlighted as lying at the heart of more resilient individuals are outlined as follows.

Seven Key Traits of Resilience

1. Emotional Awareness or Regulation

Many people believe that resilient people are tough creatures that keep their emotions under lock and key and weather the storm. The reality is different. Resilient people are actually comfortable with their emotions and express them. They are acutely aware of their feelings and are comfortable sharing them with people whom they trust. Their feelings during their challenges do not prevent them from coping and planning solutions. They do feel sad, anxious or scared, but do not become engulfed by these emotions. This ability to identify feelings and, when necessary, the ability to control them is a major factor of resilience.

Sometimes people become so overwhelmed by emotions that they find it difficult to think straight. I have met many people who admit that they do not know how they feel. Women tend to be better than men at naming their feelings. We need to acknowledge the consequences of crises on our emotions. I remember speaking to Lindsey when her mother was dying of cancer. It was a heartbreaking and draining experience for her as she watched her mother fade away. She was very busy travelling the country but she told me that sometimes out of nowhere sadness would creep up on her. 'I remember tears streaming down my cheeks while in the thick of morning city traffic,' she told me. 'It was a Friday and I had started thinking about my mother's predicament.' Fridays were customary evenings for Lindsey and her family to eat out. However, she postponed that evening's plans. She did not feel not up for the meal. She explained this to her partner – knowing that she rarely put two bad days back to back. So they rescheduled the meal for the next day. This is an example of being aware of our emotions and regulating them. Being aware of our emotions helps guide us to make better decisions. It also is a precursor to our making allowances for our vulnerability.

2. Impulse Control

Reivich suggests that resilient people are less likely to panic. They have the ability to stop and think. When we are under pressure we can experience impulses to say and do things. Resilience is not about curbing these impulses but stopping ourselves from acting on every impulse that we have. Resilient people tend not to be pushed or rushed into making the wrong decision. They will not be governed by their emotions. After addressing the group of 400 distressed people a number of years ago, I was chatting over tea and coffee with some financial consultants and barristers when a farmer approached one of the consultants. He grabbed my associate's arm and whispered loudly into his ear, 'I'm in a much better place now. I owe less money than when I was speaking to you last.' The financial consultant expressed delight but before he could ask what had changed over the six-month period, the farmer continued, 'I sold the farm. I was never going to get its value but I owe a lot less money now and the weight on my back has lessened.'

When the farmer had left the room, the consultant said to another colleague, 'That's the one thing he shouldn't have done. He's left now with three apartments and no income. He won't be able to strike any deal with the banks.' We are vulnerable to making the wrong decisions when we are emotionally distressed. The worst possible decision is often made solely through being made at the worst possible time. The resilient person can cope with the ambiguities of life and wait until their situation becomes much clearer before making major life decisions.

3. Causal Analysis and Flexibility

Resilient people seem to learn from their experiences and will take time to assess the dynamics of any given crisis. They can view their problems from different perspectives. When a resilient person fails to do well on a task, they are willing to explore factors that may have influenced the poor outcome. This flexibility allows for potential solutions to be explored.

Sometimes problems are exacerbated by an unwillingness to consult with people who potentially know more than us. I have often encountered what I term 'Know-all-ism' and this really frustrates progress when it comes to resolving issues. It also stunts growth and development. In order for us to learn from life experiences, we need to be open-minded. I have met people who know why I cannot help them before I even try.

In crisis, we need to seek as many views as possible to help inform a sound decision. Resilient people have an ability to dissect and analyse the causes of their problems and aim to seek solutions. It is important to learn from our mistakes. Resilient people build solid foundations for handling future crisis by learning from past challenges.

4. Empathy

Reivich identified empathy as a key attribute of resilient people. Empathy allows us to read and understand the emotions of others. This helps us build relations and provides social support. Crucially, resilient people are connected with others. They are not 'solo artists' in crisis but tend to lean on others for support. Empathy is an important component of strong social relationships and facilitates these strong relationships.

Stress can sometimes make us feel as if we are the only person experiencing challenge, but thinking like this does not help. The truth is that we often fail to recognise other people's worries in the midst of our own turmoil.

I remember speaking to a woman grieving the death of her husband and she said the greatest regret she had during that period was not being properly in tune with how his death had affected their children. They internalised their own grief and it was only years later that they all agreed that they could have supported each other more. At the gathering of financially distressed borrowers, the greatest tonic they received was not derived from anything in my presentation but from realising that they were not alone. Hundreds of other people were experiencing similar stress, and worse. Sometimes people mistakenly perceive resilient people as being heartless or made of stone. In fact, resilient people reach out to others and avail of any support and love that is offered. They do not 'soldier on' alone.

5. Self-Efficacy

Resilient people have confidence in their ability to solve problems. This is not an unfounded cockiness but rather an acute awareness of their inner resources. They believe in their effectiveness to help themselves and others through the crisis. It may be a person's sense of humour, creative disposition or organisational skills that are the foundations of this self-belief. They know their strengths and how best to utilise them.

We all have an innate capacity to cope better than we may realise, but resilient people know this through experience. They learn from previous difficult periods and draw confidence from what they did that helped them through those times. That ability to remember calms their nerves and makes them more resolved to carry on.

Reivich refers to this as 'self-efficacy' and claims that it is different than self-esteem, being more to do with what she calls a 'skills-based mastery set of skills for coping'. Any committee with a problematic agenda craves a leader to instil confidence. In sport, the team facing the biggest game of their season needs a manager who can remind them of, and focus them on, their strengths. This will drive them forward. Knowing your strengths and tapping into them will carry you through testing times.

6. Reaching Out and Grasping Change

Resilient people are willing to take risks to resolve problems. They are not afraid of failure. They will contemplate new ideas and not only open their minds to new concepts or approaches to problems, but also test out strategies. Sometimes the fear of failure prevents us from seeing potential solutions. We will never know if something will succeed unless we try. I have addressed business people who are afraid of change although change may be exactly what they need to survive. In a recession-stricken world, those who survive and indeed thrive in the face of adversity are those who did things differently and did different things. Often the less resilient people are more conservative in their approach, and being overly cautious can sometimes prevent us from finding solutions.

7. Optimism

A little bit of optimism goes a long way. My father was a very optimistic man. He understood my right to worry about whatever I worried about, but always insisted that things would work out. To a degree, things do tend to work out. We may not find the solution we had hoped for, but many of us eventually compromise, adjust and adapt. Resilient people do not deny their problems or believe that they never make mistakes, But they have an ability to see themselves and their situations as optimistically as they can.

Reivich advocated for an optimism that was 'wed to reality'. Imagine if all the members of a management committee were pessimistic about the prospects of their company surviving a setback. The company would be doomed. But even a shade of optimism might create an opportunity to contemplate or devise a solution not previously considered.

Reivich showed how people's optimism can be tracked in line with how they explain their failures and successes. An optimistic person who wins a competition will remind us of their efforts and hopes if speaking of their win. A pessimistic person may dismiss victory as something that surprised them or something that they cannot understand, especially considering the high standard of the other entrants.

Optimistic people tend to translate failure as a temporary setback and move on. They are keen to enter the competition again the following year and work harder at it. The pessimist may see failure as 'typical' of their misfortune and decide not to enter such competitions again.

Of the seven skills of resilience as outlined by Reivich, optimism is the most important. Her colleague Martin Seligman has shown that we can learn to be more optimistic. So there is hope for pessimists. At this juncture I want to remind you again that pessimism is not all bad: a pessimist is more likely to see the small print of the deal that seems too good to be true. They may be better prepared for the realities of failure as they were expecting it. But there can be no denying of the need for optimism during challenging times. It can help drive us forward.

I have met many resilient people through the course of my work as a psychologist and in preparation for this book. Such conversations have two effects on me. These people and their life situations remind me of how blessed I am by comparison, but they also profoundly inspire me.

When I met Kathleen again, whose husband and son had died within a year of each other, she had recently been promoted to a senior management position in her job. She was, however, still adamant that her life would never be the same again. She was also at pains to explain that she did not believe time was a 'healer', but that with time we do grow stronger. She had resumed work within a month of her husband's death. 'I knew I had to return for my own sanity,' she explained. 'I had my children and I had to be strong for them.'

She outlined how she had felt herself 'slipping' and needed the distraction of work. 'I was crying a lot, experiencing sleeplessness, eating less, not looking after myself properly and withdrawing socially from my family and friends. I was almost defined by my depressed mood.' Kathleen seemed to be inspired to do all the right things in a crisis. She eventually reconnected with her friends and soaked up the love and support of her family. She explained, 'I was blessed with offers of support and I took people up on those offers. I needed their support.' One of the best decisions she made was due to the insistence of a friend: she joined the local bridge club. She had to learn how to play and spent nearly four hours every second Tuesday night immersed in it. It acted as great distraction, but she said she often felt that some people made inappropriate judgments about her. 'They might have seen me out in the pub laughing on a Tuesday night. They might have wondered why I wasn't at home, mourning.' The truth is that Kathleen still cries herself to sleep most nights. She will always be grieving, but her life might continue for another 40 years. She has to rise to that challenge.

In rereading what I have written here, I am conscious that many people would find it difficult to react like Kathleen but I include her in this chapter because her life demonstrates how some people can manage crisis very effectively, though always remaining human and vulnerable.

9| people need people

'Depression's greatest friend is solitude and you don't have to live on your own to experience that – you just detach yourself from the people you are living with.'
—Shane Martin

We are many decades into a digital age. More and more people communicate using social networking sites, with a corresponding reduction in face-to-face contact. In Ireland, over 90 per cent of the population has at least one social-media profile and time spent on such platforms is increasing each year. It is clear that people of all ages are becoming more disengaged from each other. Whether it is texting, tweeting, using Snapchat or simply talking on the phone, sitting on the bus with earphones, using a laptop or iPad at the dinner table, electronic media has proliferated in every space and corner. It is becoming harder to experience everyday face-to-face communication. Couples spend less time in each other's company. Although they may be in the same house, they may be in different rooms using different digital platforms. A growing number of people work from home and consequently find themselves socially detached from colleagues.

One could often be excused for thinking that the television has practically displaced the parental role. A study in Britain by the Children's Society has shown that the box in the corner (or in the bedroom) eclipses 'by a factor of five or ten the time parents spend actively engaging with children'. Another ongoing study by the society reports that 25 per cent of British five-year-olds own a computer or laptop of their own. Psychologist Aric Sigman (2007) found that children spend more time in the family home alone in front of a television/computer screen than doing anything else. Parents are spending less time with their children, and don't even have to feel guilty because their child's own preference is often for their Xbox or PlayStation. There are significant drawbacks to these changes in how we communicate. A study called *The Internet Paradox* (Kraut *et al.*, 1998) examined 73 families and found that greater use of the Internet was associated with declines in communication between family members in the home, declines in their social circle, and increases in our levels of depression and loneliness.

A sociological study by McPherson and colleagues at Arizona and Duke universities in 2006 showed how the modal number of close confidants (i.e. people with whom we are comfortable sharing a personal problem) for Americans has decreased in recent decades. In 1985, most Americans had at least three confidants. In 2004 it had dropped to one. Even more astonishingly, roughly 25 per cent of those interviewed had no confidant. That would mean that one in four of the US population has no one to confide in – no close friend. Gauging by this study, loneliness would seem to be almost epidemic there. This increase in isolation and alienation may be a factor in why Americans access counselling in such vast numbers.

Without a similar study being conducted in Ireland, it is hard to ascertain whether such an increase in people seeking counselling has occurred here, too, but it seems certain that we have reduced intimacy within our communities. Many people feel that houses are closer to each other but that people are further apart. The Office for National Statistics in Britain (Ruston, 2003) revealed that people spend approximately 50 minutes a day in face-to-face contact with other people, raising questions about how the rest of our waking hours are spent.

Science has emphatically shown that social relationships – both quality and quantity – affect mental health, health behaviour, physical health and mortality risk. The most striking evidence comes from prospective studies of mortality across industrialised nations. James S. House and colleagues have shown that the people with the lowest level of involvement in social relationships are more likely to die than those with the greatest level. Another study by Lisa F. Berkman and S. Leonard Syme in 1979 showed that men and women with the fewest social ties have twice as high a risk of death in comparison to those with the most social ties. This was found to be the case even when socio-economic status, health behaviours and other variables that might influence outcomes were taken into account. Julianne Holt-Lunstad and colleagues, in their meta-analytic review 2010, confirmed that the influence of social relationships on risk for mortality was comparable with well-established risk factors for mortality. Adults who are more socially connected are healthier and live longer.

I have often expressed the view that the greatest friend of depression is solitude. And you don't have to live alone to experience it – all you have to do is detach yourself from people that you love. Many people don't tell others how they feel, or they feel there is no point, i.e. that they wouldn't be understood, or they fear being a burden. But we should never cut ourselves off from the powerful resource of company. Of course, we all need a little solitude now and again – time to think. And there may be people within our social circle who do not lift our spirits. I am not suggesting for one moment that we should spend extra time with such people. However, the reality is that we humans need each other. We need to sustain our friendships by investing in them. If we have allowed friendships to fade, we can reignite them. A quick phone call may be needed to reacquaint us. But we need to keep them alive through fostering them with effort and time.

A few years ago I enrolled my son in the boarding school that I had attended myself. Emotionally, I was taken aback by the experience. I bumped into people I hadn't seen since doing the Leaving Certificate. Like me, they were enrolling their own sons. I even bumped into a couple of teachers who had taught me all those years ago. I felt a real sense of nostalgia. The corridors had the same smell. The stairs, doors, windows were all unchanged and ghosts from my past were everywhere. Memories bubbled to life.

People can feel lonely when they count or list their number of friends. They realise that it may have been years since they met some of them. The friendship is no longer there – only memories of it. It can be a pity to let some friendships fade away altogether. It's remarkable how you can turn the chapters back and catch up on the story.

Life is busy, but sometimes we should simply make a better effort with our friendships. We have to work at keeping them alive. Of course, it can be difficult to rekindle a lost friendship; it may even be impossible. But there is nothing to lose by attempting to re-establish a connection. I was invited to a gathering of six school friends just before Christmas. It fell on a day that didn't really suit me. It meant a long journey after a hard day's work. But, being acutely aware that these invitations are rare, I made the long journey and had one hell of a night.

As we settle into a marriage or long-term partnership, or when children arrive, we can lose the habit of inviting people to our homes. We can also get into the habit of turning invitations down. I have often maintained that we can become very boring as we grow older. Friendships, past and present, are treasures. We should celebrate them as much as we can.

We should also leave ourselves open to forming new friendships. We could benefit from getting involved in our communities through volunteering, clubs, activities, etc. If the greatest friend of depression is solitude, where you just listen to your own self-damning theories without interruption or without the voice of reason being in the room, the greatest enemy of self-inflicted negativity is distraction. We get lots of distraction by being social. I remember a middle-aged woman who told me that she regretted the choice she had made in moving to a particular town: people were unfriendly and she had made no friendships in over twenty years. It was almost as if she had a theory about the place – as if a different type of human being lived there. As she continued, I couldn't stop thinking about a friend of mine who lives in the same town. Over the years he has always spoken of its inhabitants as being wonderfully warm and hospitable people. He described a completely different town, with plenty to do, a rich artistic tradition and great sporting facilities. It left me wondering about what efforts she had made to become part of the community.

There was a time when we Irish were famous for our welcome. The phrase *céad míle fáilte* (one hundred thousand welcomes) was a mantra for Irish people. We were good at talking; storytelling was our forte. On dark winter evenings we sat around the fire to reminisce and imagine. The surprise visitor added intrigue to the evening. We went to see neighbours when they were in hospital. We welcomed new neighbours moving in. We called on the bereaved to see how they were doing. We kept an eye on the lonely souls of our community.

I'm not saying that we have completely stopped all this, but there seems to have been a significant decline in meaningful social connection in recent decades. I have met many people on my travels who raise this as a very real issue, particularly in rural Ireland, but a sense of isolation can be found everywhere.

How many families connect with each other in a meaningful way? I remember observing a family at a large table in a restaurant in Sligo: a mother and father; a granny; three teenage girls in the local convent uniform; two children in primary-school uniforms; and a twenty-something individual. Nine members of the same tribe gathered for a feast, six of them with devices in their hands. There was evident tension when the mother pressed one of the teenagers to choose from the menu: 'You pick for me, Ma. Something like Chicken Kiev.' Her answer eased the tension. Her mother could now speak to the waitress on her daughter's behalf. Her daughter's insistence on using her mobile device meant that she hadn't even read the menu. During the meal it was very clear that little or no conversation was taking place. They seemed well skilled in negotiating between knives, forks and buttons.

Children need to learn to be social, particularly as it is a life skill clearly linked to better health outcomes. There is a couple that I know with two very noisy and demanding children of around the same age. Any time I had visited, there was a wrestling match between the children, or between them and one of their parents. It was hard to develop flowing conversation with these constant interruptions. The mother once asked me whether I thought they were hyperactive. In truth, I saw them as children being children – competing for our attention. But there was always tension in the room because of the constant interruption by the children.

My visit to the same house after Christmas last year was a dramatically different experience. We adults got to chat properly. I assumed that the energetic twosome were with neighbours or simply asleep. I was wrong. When I queried their absence, I was informed that Santa had solved the problem: the children were in their bedrooms on their new tablets. The mother did state that they would be careful about not allowing them stay too long on their new devices. But I wondered about two busy people returning from work every evening, longing for peace and quiet. It could be very tempting to promote the use of the same tablets.

As a child, I often walked with my family about two miles from Carrickmacross out the Shercock Road to my grandparents' house. We chatted and laughed as we followed the twisting road to the warm welcome that awaited. As a teenager I listened attentively to my grandfather's memories of his Ireland and his opinions on politics and sport. My father also often brought me with him on what was known as 'the rounds'. Usually on Saturdays, we'd call to certain houses in the countryside to collect blocks for the fire, turnips or carrots for the dinner, or to the blacksmith to see my father's horse shod. I was often asked to throw my accordion in the boot of the car in case a tune was needed; I often visited sick people with my father too and played for them. The experience stood to me many years later as I had learned how to be social with people outside my own social zone at school. It's vitally important that children connect with their community.

Today's children are experiencing less social interaction and fewer connections during key stages of their psychological, emotional and physical development. In 1998 researcher Robert E. Kraut reported that increased use of the internet was associated with declines in communication between family members and a reduction in social circles. They also reported social disengagement and worsening of mood; limited face-to-face social interaction leads to a poorer quality of life, and diminished physical and psychological health as a consequence. I commend school projects that link children to their communities: transition year offers teenagers the chance to experience the world of work, and opportunities to work alongside adults in shops, restaurants or factories. A shy girl may develop more confidence from her social exchanges with a 53-year-old woman in Tesco doing work experience than six years of secondary school.

We cannot rewind time; life moves on, and technological advances have many positives. For instance, a previous employer of mine offers clients with social phobia a development course through Skype. Counselling over the Internet has the potential to help such people build up their confidence and eventually maybe even leave their homes to face the counsellor in a more traditional setting. And there is no doubt that social-media platforms like Facebook, Twitter and Snapchat can help keep us in touch.

But we need to be very careful that we do not disconnect ourselves from our greatest resource – each other. Through social media platforms we are connecting through a digital interface. This is better than not connecting at all. But we need to ensure that it is not replacing too much face-to-face human connection. By visiting friends, joining clubs, volunteering, attending social functions and welcoming new neighbours to our estate or road, we form key human bonds. These foster a stronger sense of community. Science indicates that we need face-to-face contact and intimate human connections in order to engage the biological systems that have evolved for millennia to preserve our well-being.

I have been privileged to hear many life stories. Often these stories are underpinned by a deep-rooted loneliness. People share details of their crises and the psychological impact on the quality of their lives with me. They express the relief they feel from offloading their problems during therapy. Many of these people readily admit that they have no one else to turn to. But much of modern-day loneliness is unnecessary.

As we grow older, our social networks can shrink. Maybe, as I have already suggested, it has something to do with settling down into a marriage or long-term relationship, and being employed full-time. Many couples commute long hours and return from work exhausted. Sometimes the last thing we feel like doing is entertaining visitors or going to visit people ourselves. We're too busy. Too tired. Our friends scatter as they settle down in other parts of the country or the world. And it takes effort to become acquainted with a new community. Sometimes it feels like too much. Someone in their early fifties told me recently that they hadn't the energy to make new friends. However, the truth is that we need these relationships.

Two Christmases ago, I bought myself a Nespresso machine. I love coffee and, when a friend demonstrated his prized possession, I felt compelled to invest in one myself. Now, at the touch of a button, in the comfort of my home, I can enjoy an Americano, latte or cappuccino. I drink less coffee when I travel because the quality of my coffee at home is superior. Over a decade ago, at a time when pubs were still very busy, I remember a conversation with friends about the growing number of off-licences around the country. These were perceived as a threat to the future of the traditional Irish pub. One friend argued that the future of the pub was secure because a pint of creamy Guinness was something that could only be found in the pub. The bottled Guinness at the off-licence was an old man's drink, he said, and it didn't taste as good as the black stuff from the tap. A few years later Guinness launched a new can with a patented widget that helped maintain a head on the stout. Arguably, there was no need to go to the pub for a cool creamy Guinness anymore.

When banks introduced ATMs many people observed that this technology would remove the need for queues at counters. We believed then that the hole-in-the-wall would never completely remove the need to deal with real people because money could not be lodged through them. Now you can lodge cheques and cash without interacting with a staff member at any stage of the transaction. With the advent of Internet banking, the need to interact with human beings has decreased even further.

The video store has closed. You can download films from your sofa through Netflix or iTunes. Only a handful of record shops have weathered the storm, as downloading is now the norm for music purchases, too. We can interact online with people we don't know and will never meet. We no longer need to congregate around the television for our news as we are updated throughout the day on our own devices. And what about our local bookshops? We are witnessing their demise too as Amazon and other online resources vacuum up the book market.

I am not an old fogey: it's not that I want to halt the technological revolution or curb innovative ideas. But I am conscious that more and more of our everyday chores are becoming the stuff of pressing buttons or clicking a mouse. More and more hours are spent at home doing things on our own.

Scientific studies into life satisfaction tell us that people need people. We still need to connect to each other. It's important that we legislate for this vital connection while it's ever-easier to become detached and harder to remain connected. Maybe the spirit of community life in Ireland is fading away. Maybe the more we connect to technology, the more we disconnect from people in a real sense.

This is very evident in our work relationships. I remember speaking to someone who was deeply hurt because some colleagues hadn't attended her father's funeral or even acknowledged his death on her return to work afterwards. The truth is that by building more positive relationships (at any level), we will potentially create a happier work environment. When you talk to people who say they are happy in their work, it is nearly always the case that there is a healthy social dimension to their job.

However, sometimes we have to work with difficult people – people who are not that friendly themselves. We cannot all get on with each other. Arguments and disagreements are part of the reality within our world of communication. We can have our toes stood on and we can tread on the toes of others. Many people ask me for advice about this so I have compiled a list of ten tips for how to handle 'difficult' people, which I hope may be helpful.

Top Tips for 'Difficult' People

1. Remind yourself that sometimes we haven't a clue about what's going on in other people's lives. Some people are genuinely not at their best.

2. Many people are not blessed with warm personalities. Their words or actions may not be personal.

3. Remain mannerly, friendly and polite. Meeting rudeness with rudeness only doubles the rudeness, and doesn't make you feel better.

4. Apply empathy. Try to step into the shoes of the difficult person and imagine the world from their perspective. By reaching out to people, offering our help, support or encouragement, we can potentially transform relationships.

5. Loving the lovable is easy. Loving those who seem unlovable is a challenge. But science confirms that reaching out in compassion helps you and the person at the receiving end. Kindness can be a precursor to solutions.

6. If you have been treated harshly by a difficult person, all you can do is communicate this to them. You have no control over how they will respond. You may have to accept that they will not even meet you halfway. Remember that such intransigence is ultimately doing them more harm than it is doing you.

7. Forgiveness sets us free. It's hard but it's worth working on it.

8. Sometimes we cannot fix things. We can only make the best sense of the situation and move on. If you have genuinely tried to get on with the difficult person to no

avail, you may have to work at moving on. Talking and thinking about it less will help. Reminding yourself that you need to do this will make it easier.

9. Sometimes we may be part of the problem. Maybe our words or actions were misinterpreted by an overly sensitive person. We may have to investigate this possibility.

10. If the difficult person is really upsetting you to the degree that it affects the quality of your life, you may need to get professional advice on how to handle the specific situation.

In conclusion, we should decide to connect better and more often with others. We need people in our lives.

Research has confirmed that there is a direct connection between social isolation, loneliness, and an increasing vulnerability towards poor health. It seems that people need people. Through connecting with each other we sustain better health outcomes.

John Cacioppo, a social psychologist and neuroscientist at University of Chicago, has studied the biological effects of loneliness and has found that it is linked to dramatic increases in the stress hormone cortisol, hardening of the arteries (which leads to high blood pressure), inflammation in the body, and can diminish executive functioning e.g. learning and memory.

Human beings are social creatures – we need to connect with each other. This social connectivity is needed to maintain physical health and longevity.

Some Tips for Increased Social Connectivity

1. Start at home. How many families sit at a table for dinner anymore? We need to connect better with the people we love: Ask them how they are doing. Enquire about the kind of day that they've had. Often family members can be found eating their own dinner in their own room in front their own screen!

2. Ensure that there is a boundary between work and home. I have met people who regret not having got to know their children while they were growing up. Some people come home from work and start more work. Social connectivity is often a victim of overwork.

3. Families need to do more things together at home. With technology, family members can find themselves doing more of their own things on their own. We can become locked into our own worlds. Plan social events for family – weekends away (i.e. visiting relatives), picnics, walks, funfairs, etc.

4. Ensure that you have at least one room with no television in it. This should be the room dedicated to a lit fire and conversation.

5. Invest in friendships. Often people talk about how they are blessed with a life-long friend. But sometimes there is little or no real social connection involved. We need to visit our friends and have them over to our homes. We need to plan social events together. This demands effort as we live busy lives. But just because you are unsuccessful at gathering friends together doesn't mean that you should not try again.

6. Be open to developing new friendships. Sometimes we sit beside the same people at work. We fail to offer a warm welcome or helping hand to a new member of staff. We should show an interest in all members of the team and avoid setting up exclusive cliques. There may be a wonderful new friend on the staff whom you haven't got to know yet.

7. Volunteer! Offer your talents and support to a local charity and meet and work with new people. This will mean that you will engage in new conversations about new things – which will refresh your mind.

8. Accept as many kind invitations to parties or social gatherings as possible when the alternative is to lie on the sofa watching shows on television.

10| mind your body

'Good for the body is the work of the body,
good for the soul is the work of the soul,
and good for either the work of the other.'
—Henry David Thoreau

Exercise

When I was growing up in Carrickmacross, we had one television. It was in the living room. The second channel came on in the evening. Some of the British channels were available but reception was very poor. The TV was switched on for the nightly news bulletin. The family often sat together for a film, particularly at Christmas. There was no remote control. Sometimes tension arose over who should get up to switch channels, or change the volume. If there was any hint of a row between the Martin siblings, my parents turned the TV off. It was as simple as that. And if my father thought that we were watching too much television, he would unplug the fuse in the fuse box.

This didn't happen that often. The truth of it was that there wasn't much on the television to capture our imaginations for long. Because there was only one TV set in the corner, we had to compromise on our preferences. Now it's different. Children can watch what they want as often as they want on a handheld device. Most children now don't need to leave their bedrooms to find entertainment. Many have their own television in their own room.

Research indicates that children are becoming heavier. We have a growing problem with obesity in Ireland according to a national longitudinal study of children (Williams *et al.*, 2009). Studies show that increasing numbers of children throughout the world are being treated for depression. One of the most effective treatments for alleviating depressive symptoms is daily exercise. It's free and helps us release our own inner anti-depressants, but people in general are probably exercising less than at any time in mankind's history.

Evidence is emphatic about the health benefits of keeping a regular exercise regime. It is good for the mind and body. Exercising regularly lowers your risks of developing many serious illnesses, including stroke and heart disease. By strengthening our muscles and shedding excess weight, our bodies can work better. Science also confirms that regular exercise reduces high blood pressure, some cancers, type 2 diabetes, osteoporosis and obesity. There is no doubt that becoming more active and sustaining a daily exercise routine will improve your health and quality of life. Regular exercise should be an immediate priority and something to get working on right away if your current lifestyle includes little or none.

Exercise Energises You and Boosts Mood

We may not always feel like a brisk walk or a visit to the gym. Sometimes we come home from a hard day's work and just want to crash on the couch. But if you could be persuaded to try some exercise, you would feel energised, and might avoid returning to the couch afterwards. Exercise on a regular basis leads to an increase in energy levels overall, due to an increase in cardiovascular fitness. Having some extra energy 'in storage' helps us fight fatigue and boost motivation, and leads to a general improved sense of well-being. We feel better physically but also emotionally.

Scientists have shown that exercise creates a natural chemical 'high' by releasing endorphins ('feel-good' chemicals). Exercise also releases or 'burns off' excess adrenaline, which, in oversupply, contributes to stress. Exercise also affects serotonin levels. Serotonin contributes to a range of functions, including appetite, libido, sleep and mood. Regular exercise can alter serotonin levels, resulting in improved mood, a sense of well-being and reduced levels of depression. Studies show that the effect of exercise is immediate and can last up to twelve hours. Best results are reported from exercise taken on a daily basis.

We often become stuck in a cycle of worry. Exercise is an excellent form of distraction. The more we think about our problems, the more anxious we become or remain. After a bad day at work, we may feel that all our energy has evaporated. Removing yourself from your desk, from a stressful home situation or from a cycle of continuous anxious thinking by going for a walk or swim, or some other form of exercise, can prove the ideal tonic. You will definitely feel much better afterwards. But don't bring your problems with you. If you have a tendency to stew over your worries, it could be better to bring some company with you. The company may help distract you and ensure that the potential benefits of the exercise are not hampered by you bringing your anxiety along.

The Social Aspect to Exercise

Exercise can also be a social outlet with potentially very positive psychological effects. If you play a sport, or become a member of a gym, you will meet other people. You could plan to meet with friends or family for a walk, or join an exercise class or running group. Exercise can help build confidence and self-esteem. As we feel fitter and stronger, we will also feel more content – knowing that we are investing in our health. This produces a new confidence and a sense of satisfaction. Often people transform from being worried about their appearance and excessive weight to celebrating feeling and looking better. People who exercise often are happy about the fact that they do. They know it is good for them and this makes them feel good within themselves.

Exercise can produce a real sense of achievement. Fitness is an excellent area to set targets and goals and to follow a path to achieving them. Such goals keep us motivated and when we join with others working towards achieving common goals, it can prove easier to persist. It is noticeable that more and more people are jogging regularly. Such people often cite that being part of a group is a key motivating factor. Belonging to a weekly jogging club allows you to form the habit of regular exercise. I know two brothers who have gone for a walk together at 7 a.m. every day all of their adult lives: that's every day for nearly 40 years. They formed a walking habit – a good habit to form. Not everyone can form such a 'huge' habit but even a variation on or more modest version of this would have enormous health benefits. We can get ourselves into a rut and start to believe that we can never get around to doing what we really want to do. A daily walk is one of the best habits you can ever develop.

I remember speaking with a young man in his twenties. He was attending university and working towards a teaching qualification. He had recently experienced symptoms of depression. But as he opened up to me, I realised that he had experienced immense stress for most of his life. His father had died when he was very young and his mother was now terminally ill. A favourite uncle had been killed in the Troubles in Northern Ireland. His sister had emigrated and aspects of his study were draining him of energy. I thought to myself that he was actually doing very well considering all these setbacks. He attended his lectures and maintained a social life, while working all the time towards his goal of being a teacher.

I asked him about hobbies and learned that he went to the gym every morning and was also in a running club. I couldn't help but conclude that this structured daily exercise had stood him in good stead. Needless to say, I encouraged him to keep it up.

Some of the most depressed people take very little exercise. They lie in bed or on the couch. They maintain that they have no motivation to go for a walk. I have sometimes enlisted the help of a spouse or partner (with the client's consent) to develop a walking partnership with the person who has depression, to set a time and try to form a daily habit. The client will not feel instant benefits. They will likely be cynical about it as an intervention. But my experience is that the benefits will eventually be experienced. It takes time to reap them. The brain must become used to secreting its own natural anti-depressants. Often, what we need is not what we want.

Exercise as a Treatment for Low Mood

Science is emphatic about the physical and mental health benefits of exercise. Numerous studies show a causal link between physical activity and reduced clinically defined depression. According to the National Institute for Clinical Excellence, patients with depression, in particular those with mild to moderate depressive disorder, benefit from structured and supervised exercise. It is an effective intervention that has a clinically significant impact on depressive symptoms. A growing number of comparative studies demonstrate that exercise can be as effective as medication or therapy. And, unlike some of the anti-depressants championed throughout the world, exercise has no negative side effects.

We may wonder why doctors almost instantly prescribe anti-depressants to patients experiencing depression. The reason is that they tend to work. Some studies suggest that 68–72 per cent of people with depressive symptoms report improvement after six to eight weeks of taking anti-depressant medication. Not bad. I'd love to know more about how 'improved' they really are, but we cannot universally condemn the use of such medication. I know people who are in a much better place now as a consequence of very effective medicine. But, combined with exercise, the improvement might be even more profound.

Some studies have suggested that daily structured exercise rivals anti-depressants as an effective intervention. Sometimes doctors are criticised for over-prescribing medication as a treatment for depressed mood. But it's not as simple as them having a bias for drugs. It's not that they are ignoring the potential benefits of a daily exercise programme for their patients. Imagine if a doctor prescribed a structured daily exercise routine instead of medicine for a depressed patient – would the patient do it? It's easier to take tablets daily so there is a greater chance of compliance and improvement. Innovative general practices in the UK have an exercise coach who connects with the patient, to encourage and monitor exercise. There is also evidence that regular physical exercise sustained over time helps prevent depression.

How Much Exercise Do We Need?

The World Health Organization recommends a minimum of 150 minutes of moderate-intensity aerobic physical activity each week. This type of exercise includes activities such as a brisk walk, swimming, mowing the lawn or carrying the shopping bag home. It is also recommended that we get 75 minutes weekly of what is termed 'vigorous-intensity aerobic physical activity'. This is more intense exercise like running or aerobic dancing. Strengthening activity, like lifting weights or mountain climbing, should be incorporated into your week on at least two occasions.

The more we do, the better, but we have to start small and slowly increase our regime. The World Health Organization also recommend that children up to the age of seventeen have a minimum of 60 minutes of moderate to vigorous activity every day and strengthening three times weekly. It would be safe to conclude that the vast majority of adults and children are not adhering to these guidelines.

Sleep

Sleep requirements can vary depending on the individual and what stage they are at in life. The newborn baby spends approximately sixteen hours per day sleeping. As we grow older we require less. But we all need sleep. We all need to re-charge our batteries sufficiently in order to sustain good health, be positive and function properly. In general, most healthy adults need approximately eight hours' sleep every night but some adults can function on less. Others cannot achieve optimum performance in their day without at least ten hours. Sleep problems are quite common. Elderly people complain of sleeplessness a lot, and those over 65 are reported to have most difficulty. Some studies have indicated that up to 30 per cent of the adult population report having difficulties sleeping. Sleeplessness is often very understandable and having trouble with sleep at some stage of your life can almost be expected. If someone has ongoing problems with getting a good night's sleep, this insomnia can have significant impact on their quality of life. It is important to give ourselves every opportunity to achieve proper rest and to avoid long periods of sleeplessness.

Sleeping is a complex activity. It has no on/off switch. It is a process consisting of at least five different types or stages, varying from light to deep sleep, and can be divided into REM (Rapid Eye Movement) and non-REM sleep. We slip in and out of REM several times during the night. When we are in REM sleep, we tend to dream. Sleep experts divide non-REM sleep into four stages. The first is drowsiness – when we are just about to nod off. The second stage is sleep and the third stage is deeper sleep. The fourth stage is deep sleep – it is during this stage that we are most unlikely to be woken easily. During any given night we switch regularly between theses modes. Sometimes we can wake up fully several times.

As we grow older, the type and quality of our sleep varies. Compared to a younger person, an older person may only experience 10 per cent of deep sleep. (Typically, a young adult might spend 25 per cent of the night in the deep mode.) The older person wakes more easily, as they predominantly switch between the drowsiness mode and sleep modes. That's why, as we grow older, we wake more during the night, experience shorter periods of deep sleep, and can be more restless and more easily woken. Sleep problems can become a serious issue.

What Causes this Sleeplessness?

STRESS

Stress is considered the number one cause of short-term sleeping difficulties. Family or relationship/marital discord, bereavement, worrying about your health, financial stresses or job-related pressures can lead to periods of disturbed sleep. Usually when these stressful events or periods pass, better sleep patterns return. A stressful day almost always leads to poorer-quality sleep that night. An ongoing stressful situation or worry is often at the heart of sleeplessness. We often find ourselves waking up worried, or find it difficult to nod off because we are running through stressful situations in our minds. Many people internalise their worries and fail to seek an opinion or advice on the issues causing them stress. They are like a shaken soda bottle ready to explode. Being overly concerned or anxious about our sleep patterns can further exacerbate the problem. Constantly monitoring our sleep, or lack of it, and watching the clock only adds to this. While ongoing broken sleep can be draining, it is important to remind ourselves that we cannot die from it.

GOING TO THE TOILET

We increasingly wake up to go to the toilet as we become older. Pregnancy is another reason for toileting during the night. After the age of 60, the vast majority of people wake up at least once a night to go to the toilet. It's important not to become anxious about interruptions like these. Sometimes people become worried about the need for toileting during the night but it is quite a normal activity as we grow older.

POOR SLEEPING ENVIRONMENT

Our environment is an influential factor in this. We sleep better in the dark; it's harder to sleep in a bright room. If the room is too hot or cold, we may find ourselves waking up. Silence aids sleep and a noisy environment will impact on our ability to sleep. It is best to leave devices like mobile phones, tablets, laptops, etc. outside the bedroom. Browsing online or answering text messages or emails forces concentration on a mind that needs to naturally tire and enter the drowsiness stage. It is even more frustrating to be awoken by a text message or tweet after falling asleep.

BEREAVEMENT

Loss and bereavement can also affect sleep. The loss of a partner, family member or close friend is a significant life event. Loneliness can wake people regularly during the night. It is important to seek support if bereavement engulfs you completely. You need to be mentally strong to deal with grief, and ongoing sleeplessness can drain vital energy for coping. Counselling can help to alleviate the pain and help you work on strategies to maintain sufficient resilience.

PHYSICAL PAIN

This is a very obvious complication to achieving a good night's rest. If someone is experiencing significant physical pain (e.g.

arthritis), they find it harder both to go to sleep and to remain asleep. Physical pain can encompass back or muscle pain, toothache or stomach cramps. I have met people who endure pain and avoid seeking help from their GP. As a consequence, they go through a sustained period of broken sleep. This continuous sleep disruption can allow their bodies to become accustomed to a poor sleep pattern. Even when the pain subsides, they are left with a major challenge in learning how to sleep again. By checking in with a GP they often find an effective remedy for the pain, which results in an increase in the likelihood of achieving better sleep.

CAFFEINE, SOFT DRINKS AND CIGARETTES

Caffeine taken hours before can affect our sleep. Preferably we need to avoid coffee, tea, hot chocolate and soft drinks for six hours before bedtime. Avoiding all drinks close to sleeping time also ensures that we go to bed without a full bladder. Cigarettes contain nicotine, which is a stimulant, so should also be avoided in the hours approaching sleeping time.

Many people wrongly believe that alcohol will help them sleep. A few strong brandies may make you feel drowsy enough to fall asleep easily, but a good night's sleep does not always follow. In fact, you are almost guaranteed to wake up. Alcohol interferes with normal sleep patterns and impacts on the quality and quantity of sleep during the course of the night. The sedative effect of alcohol may help you nod off but it leads to lower quality sleep interrupted by frequent awakenings. You will typically rise feeling unrefreshed and more tired. Technically speaking, your body recognises alcohol as poison and puts in train a series of actions to curb its effect. The chemical vasopressin is suppressed. It sends a signal to your kidneys to reabsorb water rather than sending everything to the bladder. As a consequence, you are more likely to awaken to go to the toilet than if you had not taken alcohol as your bladder fills. In the morning you will sense a degree of dehydration and experience a heavy head or headache.

POOR SLEEP ROUTINE

We are creatures of habit. Workers with early morning shifts tend to wake up early even when on holidays. Their sleeping cycle has been programmed as a consequence of the need to rise early for work. Routine aids sleep. It is recommended that you have a period of winding down in the hours before bedtime. You should avoid stressful, stimulating activities or discussing or thinking about emotional issues. Otherwise you will secrete the stress hormone cortisol, which sets your body into a state of alertness.

Relaxation techniques or meditation allow your body and mind to calm down and become more ready for sleep. Even if you are experiencing very poor sleep, it is best to stick with a consistent routine and avoid having a nap during the day.

OBSESSION WITH THE CLOCK

Sometimes wondering whether we will fall asleep or not is what has us staying awake. I have met many people who have become obsessive monitors of their sleep. In these cases it probably is best to turn your clock away from your gaze altogether.

LATE DINNERS AND TREATS

Eating a burger and chips or Chinese takeaway at 10 pm is a recipe for poor sleep. Avoid foods that disagree with you. If you have to have a snack, settle for foods that won't disrupt sleep, like dairy products and carbohydrates.

EXERCISING LATE AT NIGHT

Exercise helps us sleep but it's important not to leave it too late at night. By exercising we stimulate the cortisol hormone associated with alertness. This is fine before an exam or an important meeting, but not an hour before going to bed. It is recommended to finish exercise at least three hours before bedtime.

Diet

We know that an unhealthy diet is linked to many diseases and conditions, including obesity, diabetes and cancer. When it comes to determining a link between food and mood, the science is quite limited. There have been some studies that have suggested that omega–3 fatty acids and some minerals like selenium, zinc and magnesium might prevent mood disorders, but the findings have been inconsistent.

There are many books that concentrate on diet, but I feel we need to examine how we eat as well as what we eat. Lunch has become something that we gobble down while walking or driving. Many children eat their food as they lie on the ground while watching a screen. Fast-food is a thriving business and often we do not even know what we are eating. The recent horse-meat scandal hasn't left people fussier about the food they consume or how it was sourced or produced.

Many of us no longer even sit while we eat. We may not realise how fast we actually eat our food. When we eat quickly, we consume larger chunks of food and the stomach has more to do than it would otherwise. After a stressful day at work, we sometimes vacuum food up in a couple of minutes. We don't taste the flavours. We forget that the wars of the workplace are over, and that this is peacetime. It's remarkable how we some-times cannot even remember what we ate at all.

Eating like this is indicative of a stressful lifestyle and it would best be stopped completely. It's a right that we need to defend in an ever-more-pressurised world – to sit at a table and eat our food slowly while enjoying the flavours. Busy restaurants sometimes offer you an hour at a table. The waiter or waitress tells you that they need the table back. No matter how good the restaurant, I always decline such offers. We should have space between courses and time to remain seated as our system digests. Very stressed people nearly always have this habit of rapidly downing their food in minutes.

Eating at a table would be a good starting point for addressing this problem. You need to remind yourself that there is no hurry. You are entitled to enjoy your food. There is no need for a smartphone or laptop. You only need a knife and fork! Remind yourself to eat slowly and concentrate on the flavours. We discussed the benefits of savouring in Chapter 6 and how to make a determined effort to savour the unique flavours of every part of the dish served. Often people rise too quickly from the dinner table – get into the habit of remaining seated and allowing your digestive system to work in comfort. I remember my grandmother putting on the kettle as we finished dinner. It was customary to have a cup of tea after dinner in her house. There was less of a rush on people in those days.

11| am i here at all? introducing mindfulness into your world

'Whatever you are doing, ask yourself,
"What's the state of my mind?"'
—Dalai Lama

remember my first year in secondary school. Academically it was a disaster. The school reports were damning. Art seemed to be the only subject that I scored well in. I had promised to work harder after the Halloween review but the end of year report confirmed similar low grades. I scanned through the report card looking for something positive to retrieve during the analysis at the kitchen table. Looking at the tutor's comment at the bottom of the report I found what I was looking for. Pointing to this, I said, 'Mum, the tutor comment is good. Look here, she says I'm absent-minded.' Ridiculously, I thought the term 'absent-minded' was a compliment – I thought it meant that I was creative or something like that. My mother laughed and told me that my head was always full. When I look back on that year, I realise that I was absent-minded a lot of the time. My head was always full of thoughts. I was thinking about my comics, football cards, marbles, television shows and new albums in the charts. I used to make my own comics and I used to be thinking through the storylines as the teachers explained something on the board. I was swapping football cards with lads at the back. I was counting my pocket money over and over again. Maybe, I'd have enough for the *Roy of the Rovers* comic and two packs of football cards. I was far from focused. As I grew older I became better at removing myself from all the 'noise' and settling to pay attention and revise. Results started to improve. But my father often asked me to 'tune in'. I can still hear him saying 'Son, I'm talking to you. Can you tune in please?' Often our minds become overloaded. We can miss something very important as we attempt to do everything at once. It's not just children that have a tendency to do this.

Our minds help us learn new things, anticipate future events, remember past incidents, interpret ongoing situations and produce ideas or theories. But our minds can also become jumbled as thoughts become scattered. We can be thinking about anything other than what we are presently tasked with. What is going on around us or what we are meant to be doing can become very blurred. Ever run up the stairs to fetch something and forgot what it was? Or drive past the turn that you were meant to take? Or follow the route home without stopping for the milk? (And you actually thought of it a few times while in the car.) Or fail to remember who told you something earlier that day? Or wondered if you remembered to slam the back door shut? Did you put on the alarm? Did you switch the cooker off? You see it's not just children whose minds become overloaded. It is challenging to command some focus or attention because there are so many things competing for our attention. We seem to have so many things to do and less and less time to do them. We could be typing a letter when our mobile phone vibrates. Or watching a movie when a newsflash appears on the screen. We seem to be surrounded, if not bombarded, by ever-increasing distractions, particularly in this technological age.

Our busy minds can allow our thoughts to become entangled and fuzzed. We can find ourselves literally in a spin, more vulnerable to making mistakes or misreading events. Sometimes we can say the opposite of what we intended to say. It's as if the wiring goes all wrong. We can jump to conclusions without seeing the whole picture. We can conclude without knowing. Or go over past events again and again or agonise over future events and imagine potential disasters repeatedly. It's as if we allow ourselves to lose control. As we multi-task, it's as if everything happens without much thought at all. We all have routines to follow at home and at work and it's easy, almost natural, to just go through the motions without truly paying attention to what we do. Our minds are constantly wandering. We may eat our dinner without tasting it, look without seeing, and talk without knowing what we are saying or what was said back to us. We lose a sense of ourselves, others and our world. It's as if we switch into automatic pilot mode.

It seems quite easy to become detached from our feelings in the present moment. We can find ourselves just doing things and moving on to do other things. You could be ironing the clothes, keeping a watchful eye on the children, listening to the news headlines, watching your smart phone for an expectant text message, and keeping a eye on the pot. But you are not aware that you are tired or that your back is wet. It's too easy to become lost in the noise of every day. This approach to life means that you actually become disconnected from yourself and your world. It's as if you lose consciousness of you being present. Numerous studies have highlighted the benefits of becoming more aware, or removing yourself from this mental noise and focusing on the fact that you are here. By doing so we would become more 'mindful'.

In recent years we see mindfulness popping up everywhere. Posters advertising courses or retreats, discussion on its benefits on the radio, documentaries about its origins and practice on the television, and specialised apps on our smart phones. Teachers are learning about it, children are being taught it and doctors recommend it to their patients. This 2500-year-old Eastern tradition seems to have taken the West by storm. But are the benefits real? Is it just the latest fad? What is mindfulness?

Leading expert professor emeritus Jon Kabat-Zinn is founder and former director of the Centre for Mindfulness in Medicine at the University of Massachusetts Medical Centre. He describes mindfulness as the practice of purposely focusing our attention on the present moment – and accepting it without judgment. It's about the quality of that attention and awareness. The first part of his definition refers to active attention, which will make us more aware. The second part of his definition emphasises the present rather than the past or future, and the third part highlights that the attention is nonjudgmental. Whatever the experience is, it cannot be good or bad, right or wrong, important or not. Mindfulness involves paying attention to the external environment (i.e. sights, sounds, smells, etc.) but also awareness of bodily sensations, thoughts and feelings.

Mindfulness should not be confused with meditation, which has many different forms and styles. The objective is not to bring yourself to a higher state of consciousness or to remove yourself from the present experience, but to initiate an increased awareness of the present moment. I remember attending a meditation class and we all had to repeat a mantra over and over again in our minds. This lasted for about twenty minutes. Mindfulness is very different to this form of meditation because the focus of the meditation is to become more deeply aware and observe the constantly changing internal and external stimuli around you. Sometimes people confuse mindfulness with relaxation techniques. You may feel more relaxed as a consequence of practising mindfulness meditation but the emphasis is on becoming more accepting of whatever state the body and mind are in. It's not about trying to alter this state or forcing calmness upon yourself. It's not about putting yourself into some kind of trance. Mindfulness is about observing, connecting with and accepting the current moment without conditions.

Kabat-Zinn has conducted extensive research into the health benefits of mindfulness meditation. It was just over 35 years ago when he developed an eight-week structured programme called Mindfulness-Based Stress Reduction (MBSR) to help people suffering from chronic pain and stress-related disorders. His programme removed the practice from its Buddhist roots. By neutralising it from its faith-based context, mindfulness became accessible to more people in the West and could be standardised for research purposes. His programme consisted of a weekly two-and-a-half-hour group class (where participants would be taught a range of mindfulness exercises and practices), daily practice at home, and attendance on a one-day retreat at the end. Based upon a systematic procedure, participants develop an enhanced awareness of moment-to-moment experiences of perceptible mental processes. By promoting this greater awareness, his programme has been shown to help reduce negative affect (mood), provide more veridical perception (the direct perception of stimuli as they exist), improve vitality and enhance coping skills. The MBSR programme has been applied within schools, prisons, and hospitals. It has been implemented across the world to alleviate suffering associated with physical, psychosomatic and psychiatric disorders. Hundreds of studies confirm positive results for different conditions among different groups. Paul Grossman and colleagues conducted a meta-analysis in 2004 and concluded that MBSR may help a broad range of individuals to cope with their clinical and non-clinical problems.

Kabat-Zinn has shown that mindfulness has a positive effect on physical and psychological symptoms, as well as positive changes in health attitudes and behaviours. Advocates of its practice theorise about its other benefits, including self-control, objectivity, mood tolerance, flexibility, improved concentration and enhancements in how we relate to others and self through increasing compassion and acceptance. Many practitioners are adamant that it provides pathways to optimal states of being like insightfulness, joy, interconnectedness and compassion. Literature from the world of happiness suggests that it is a firm foundation for greater life satisfaction. People who practise mindfulness regularly are more likely to experience greater appreciation of life via increased present-moment awareness; greater productivity as a result of improved attention, and a greater sense of inner peace by practising acceptance.

In 2015 A. Rinske and colleagues systematically reviewed the evidence of effectiveness of MBSR and Mindfulness Based Cognitive Therapy (MBCT) in a variety of patient categories. They found that the evidence supported the use of both MBSR and MBCT to alleviate symptoms, both mental and physical, in the adjunct treatment of cancer, cardiovascular disease, chronic pain, depression, anxiety and disorders, and in prevention in healthy adults and children. MBCT is an offshoot of MBSR and was developed by Zindel Segal, Mark Williams and John Teasdale based on Kabat-Zinn's programme. It combines the ideas of cognitive therapy (how thinking colours mood and influences behaviour) with meditative practices. It aims to help people become acquainted with the modes of their minds that characterise mood disorders, while simultaneously learning how to develop a new relationship with them. In 2012 W.R. Marchand and colleagues examined MBSR, MBCT and Zen meditation for depression, anxiety, pain and psychological distress. While MBSR and MBCT originate from Buddhist spiritual practices, Zen is actual Buddhist tradition. In their overview of these three specific mindfulness interventions they found that MBSR and MBCT had broad-spectrum antidepressant and anti-anxiety effects. MBCT was found to be particularly effective as an adjunctive treatment for unipolar depression. Both MBSR and MBCT were also shown to be effective as adjunctive interventions for anxiety symptoms. MBSR was found to be beneficial for general psychological health and stress management in healthy individuals as well as those with mental illness. The truth is that there are thousands of studies ongoing today confirming the benefits of mindfulness techniques for numerous conditions. Once science validates a treatment for any condition, it grows as a practice worldwide. It is because of these studies that it has become the buzz-term within health and educational settings today.

There have also been a number of studies that show the effect of mindfulness meditation on the brain. Differences in the way our brains react to regular mindfulness can be observed after only eight weeks. The brain area known as the pre-frontal cortex is more active on its right side when we are upset, annoyed, angry or worried. It is the left side that is activated more when we are calm, happy and relaxed. Neuroscientist Richard Davidson measured the activation in the brains of participants who completed the MBSR programme. The activation of their brains had shifted to the left.

There have also been studies that have shown structural change in the brains of people who practice meditation over a number of years. The results of one study by Sara Lazar and colleagues, published in *NeuroReport* in 2005, showed thicker cortical regions related to attention and sensory processing in long-term meditation practitioners compared to non-meditators. These findings also suggested that meditation practice may offset cortical thinning brought on by aging.

A study in 2003 by Davidson and colleagues showed how an eight-week training course affected the brains and immune systems of individuals. There was some evidence of increased activation in the region of the brain associated with positive affect (mood), as well as evidence that the immune system would react more robustly in antibody production after meditation training.

Another study by Y. Tang and colleagues in 2007 indicated better stress regulation, as measured by a faster decrease in levels of the stress hormone cortisol following a laboratory task among Chinese students after five days of meditative practice at 20 minutes a day. These undergraduate students also reported less anxiety, depression and anger compared to a group of students who had received relaxation training.

The reality is that most of the research and literature on mindfulness has been focused on the adult population. Many advocates of its practice have highlighted potential benefits of training children in its methods. The younger the child, the easier it is for them to be mindful. This can be observed in a baby's first experiences with food. An unsupervised baby has a lot of fun when placed in the high chair with some food. They study the food intensely, touch it, squeeze it, feel it against their face and taste it – sometimes licking it off the face and fingers. The infant or toddler is an adventurer and every first experience is a novel moment. They react 'live' to each experience. They also have the capacity to react emotionally to the 'current' experience but move quickly on to the next. A child can be crying and laughing with minutes. They can switch from tantrum mode to playful mode in an instant. There is less evidence of mental noise in their minds. Their minds seem to empty out more quickly. As they grow older they seem to find this more difficult to do.

There is an alarming growth in depression among children. Anxiety and stress are common experiences in children and adolescents and there are potentially huge benefits to be reaped by teaching children mindfulness. As they grow older, children become absorbed by the routines and systems of daily living. They will be told what to do, what is right or wrong, how to behave, what time to wake up and go to bed, and how to perform tasks to the satisfaction of teacher and school. Very soon they will be 'putting in a day' rather than truly living it. Learning to be more mindful would help them counteract some of this tendency. We will never change the world and there will always be things that have to be done. With the reality of the examinations and the pressurising points race it is inevitable that children will lose sight of themselves. But learning to connect and accept the present moment is a skill that would serve them well and protect them from excessive stress. Too many students become consumed by academic challenges and are not aware of their stress levels.

It's only a matter of time before mindfulness will be integrated into primary and secondary schools everywhere. Adults can find the simple practice of this form of meditation quite challenging. We have been programmed a totally different way over the years. But children are better learners and are more open to change. Many teachers who introduced mindfulness to their classes tell me that their students love these periods and are calmer and more attentive as a result. In Ireland, the application of mindfulness within schools has commenced in places. In due course, a standardised evidence-based approach with proper support and resources will reap great benefits. There is no reason to believe that children will not benefit as much as adults do.

Neuroscientist Amishi Jha and colleagues at University of Miami have shown that mindfulness has a positive influence on intellectual skills, improving sustained attention, visuospatial memory and concentration. Studies by Richard Chambers (University of Melbourne) and Fadel Zeidan (Wake Forest School of Medicine) have highlighted similar benefits. In 2112 Katherine Weare reviewed nineteen studies of the main body of work on mindfulness relevant to school settings. These studies were small in scale and could have been conducted to a higher standard. Despite such shortcomings, she concluded that they offered promising results and, when taken together with strong support from more comprehensive studies on adult populations, suggest that children would potentially benefit from mindfulness programmes within the context of school. Benefits to emotional well-being, mental health, ability to learn and even to the physical health of children can be potentially achieved through programmes that would be enjoyable and cost-effective.

Visitacion Valley Middle School in San Francisco is one school that has experienced great benefits from integrating mindfulness periods into its timetable. This school is surrounded by drugs and gang violence. In 2006 there were 38 killings in the area. On one occasion, students stumbled upon three dead bodies in the schoolyard. In 2007 a meditation programme called Quiet Time was introduced to the students. Students sat for fifteen minutes of meditation twice a day, overseen by their teachers. All teachers at the school received special training. Within months noticed changes in students' behaviour were reported. Suspensions (which had been very common) among students aged 11–13 were reduced by 45 per cent. Two years into the programme, there was significant improvement in attendance rates too. They had improved by 98 per cent and nowadays one-fifth of its graduates enter the highly academic Lowell High School. In the past such admissions were very rare. The same programme has been incorporated into other schools because of its success in Visitacion Valley.

In the UK over 400 secondary schools offered mindfulness meditation programmes in 2014. The Department of Education has designated three schools as pioneer schools for mindfulness teaching and has invested £1m to help other schools benefit too. Professor Katherine Weare, emeritus professor at the Universities of Exeter and Southampton's mood disorder centre, is working with teachers in the UK to develop mindfulness in the schools there. Such classes can potentially help students find the focus needed to achieve their academic goals, and evidence suggests that test results improve in children who spend a few minutes meditating before they start an exam.

We all have naturally busy minds. The mind needs training in order to learn how to focus its attention on the present moment in a systematic way, while accepting whatever arises. In other words, if you sit down in a quiet room and try to meditate, you will more than likely get distracted by a thought. You may think about what you are doing (i.e. how could something as simple as this be beneficial?) or your mind may wander as you try to remember whether or not you paid a bill. Maybe, a negative thought might visit your mind and unsettle you. Mindfulness promotes an acceptance of these intrusive thoughts and suggests that we should not react to them with aversion and avoidance. We should recognise them as what they are – thoughts. This involves a conscious effort to concentrate on what is happening in each moment. The moment may include thoughts, bodily sensations, sounds from the surrounding environment, or an awareness of your breathing. Mindfulness meditation allows you to build on this type of concentration and with practice become more aware as you observe the flow of inner thoughts, emotions and bodily sensations while you meditate. The important point is not to judge these as good or bad. The objective is to avoid holding on to a particular thought, feeling or sensation, but building an awareness around the reality that these come and go. A negative thought may enter your mind and, despite trying to suppress it, it returns. But you become more aware of such thoughts as you meditate. The exercise may initially seem to unsettle rather than calm you. But with practice the experts maintain that you will become more content and have a greater level of self-awareness. You will also become more comfortable with a wider range of emotions and experiences.

There is no doubt that our minds can become very 'noisy' and meditative practices like this seem to go against the *grain* of the brain. But many thousands of people have benefited from remaining committed to the process over time. Instead of being engulfed in this mental noise you can become your own observer of it. Mindfulness helps us to distance ourselves from our thoughts and see them neutrally. By accepting whatever arises in your awareness at each moment you develop greater kindness and forgiveness toward yourself.

Mindfulness seems simple, but it's not easy and takes practice. Many people learn to meditate on their own. There are hundreds of books, online courses, DVDs, CDs and a growing number of apps on smart phones available. You could literally start today. But it demands significant discipline and daily practice is the best practice. The first thing you need to do is to set aside some time to learn various techniques. Then you will need to legislate some space in your days for its practice. You would benefit greatly from doing a good mindfulness course. This would commit you to weekly class and homework in between. Like all courses and programmes, the standard of teaching can vary, so you may have to investigate what courses are available in your area and acting on a personal recommendation would be a bonus. There is no doubt that you would benefit from the support of a teacher or instructor; you would also be able to liaise with classmates to help answer your queries, share your experiences and keep motivated. Personally I think the self-help route (doing it on your own) can be too ambitious and unrealistic for many people. If you have depression, anxiety or any other condition, it may be a good idea to speak to your GP. They may be able to refer you to a mindfulness practitioner who has experience in the practice of mindfulness to alleviate symptoms.

I remember chatting to Marcus, who was worked up about his upcoming exams. He told me that his head was overloaded. When he was studying he would be agonising over whether or not he would get sufficient material covered in the allotted tim frame. When he stopped studying, he worried about whether or not he would ever get all his revision done. Even as he spoke to me, he said that thoughts about the study he had to do later that day unsettled him. It was nearly as if our conversation was holding him back from more urgent study. The consequence for him was that he was very uptight, nervous and agitated. I remember trying some meditative techniques with him, but it was clear they were not working well. He admitted to me that he found it hard to be still in the moment.

The following week I organised the room in a specific way to enhance an exercise that I intended to practice with him. I placed a vase of lilies on the bookshelf, a small ticking clock on the mantelpiece, left a radio on low volume in the room next door, and left the window slightly ajar to let the sounds from outside enter. He arrived and took his seat. I asked him, 'Do you notice anything different about this room?' He scanned it very quickly and pointed to the table. 'You polished the table!' he replied. The truth was that I hadn't actually touched the table. I asked him to sit more comfortably in the chair, allowing the soles of his feet to touch the ground. I then asked him to sit still for two minutes. The exercise was for him to concentrate on his surroundings – listening attentively for any sounds he could hear, to become aware of odours, to be sensitive to sensations in his body and so on. If thoughts about study intruded it was okay: 'Just re-focus,' I advised him, 'and return to this room.' When he opened his eyes, the first words he uttered were, 'Where are the lilies?' He then listed out the sounds he heard and turned his attention to the clock and opened window. The exercise worked a treat and he loved it. I reminded him that he could connect with the world while on a walk in the forest, overlooking a city from a balcony, or watching the tide ease out from a beach.

If you are reading this sentence, why not try to connect with this moment in a very real way? How are your holding this book? Is your hand strained? What are you sitting on? Is it comfortable? What position are you legs in? Is one crossed over the other? Can you sense where they touch? Is the room warm? Can you smell anything right now? And what about your body? Do you have any aches or pains in this moment? Are the muscles around your shoulders tight or relaxed? Is your stomach full or empty? Is it making sounds? It is possible to connect better with our world, but you nearly have to remind yourself to do so. Forming a daily habit of regularly connecting in a mindful way with your surroundings like this would potentially be beneficial for you. Maybe set a reminder on your phone. You could also decide to be the last person to retire to bed each night. Before you switch off the last light you could take a few minutes to meditate.

Remember mindfulness is a deep awareness of the present moment. It is about living in the here and now. Through mindfulness meditation you free yourself from the past and the future because you concentrate only on what IS. Great inner peace will come from focusing all your attention on what is happening right now.

It takes practice because our minds are not accustomed to being quiet. Our body's inner biology is used to adrenaline and cortisol pumping at regular intervals every day. As we practise stillness, we become distracted. It's almost as if we are doing something unnatural. It's a bit like driving on the other side of the road when you travel abroad. It seems wrong. Our system nearly wants to autocorrect. But do not allow the tendency to adjust (or get back to the 'noise') discourage you from the practice. Keep returning to the moment that is NOW. I remember speaking with an expert practitioner and he recommended that I practise the 'one-minute' mindfulness exercise.

'Everyone can do the one-minute exercise,' he said. 'If you

were to practise it every day and extend its duration slowly to ten minutes, you would possibly transform your approach to life.'

One-Minute Mindfulness Exercise

This is an easy mindfulness exercise, and one that you can do any time throughout the day. Take a moment right now to try. Check your watch and note the time. For the next 60 seconds, your task is to focus all your attention on your breathing. It's just for one minute. Find your breath. Tune into the natural rhythm of your breathing. Don't hurry it or slow it down. Just become aware of it – this gift of life within you. Focus on each breath as you inhale and exhale. Leave your eyes open and breathe normally but count each individual breath. Don't worry if you miss one or become distracted. Just return to the exercise.

This mindfulness exercise is far more powerful than you might think. Use it many times throughout the day to restore your mind to the present moment, and to restore your mind to clarity and peace. Over time, you can gradually extend the duration of this exercise into longer and longer periods. This exercise is the foundation of a correct mindfulness meditation technique.

references

2. THINKING STRAIGHT

Burns, D. (1999) *The Feeling Good Handbook*, Plume.

3. WE NEED FLOW IN OUR LIVES: AT HOME AND IN THE WORKPLACE

Csikszentmihalyi, M. (1998) *Finding Flow: The Psychology of Engagement with Everyday Life*, Basic Books.

Csikszentmihalyi, M. (2008) *Flow: The Psychology of Optimal Experience*, Harper Perennial Modern Classics.

4. CULTIVATING COMPASSION

Allen, J.P.; Philliber, S.; Herrling, S.; and Kuperminc, G.P. (1997) 'Preventing Teen Pregnancy and Academic Failure: Experimental Evaluation of a Developmentally Based Approach', *Child Development*, 68(4): 729–742.

Batson, D., and Shaw, L. (1991) 'Evidence of Altruism: Toward a Pluralism of Prosocial Motives', *Psychological Inquiry*, 2(2): 107–122.

Benson, P.L.; Gil Clary, E.; and Scales, P. (2007) 'Altruism and Health: Is There a Link During Adolescence?' in Post, S. (ed.), *Altruism and Health: Perspectives from Empirical Research*, Oxford University Press.

Benson, P.L., and Roehlkepartain, E.C. (1993) *Learning to Serve, Serving to Learn*, Abingdon Press.

Davidson, R.J., *et al.* (2004) 'Long-Term Meditators Self-Induce High-Amplitude Gamma Synchrony During Mental Practice', *Proceedings of the National Academy of Science*, 101(46): <http://www.pnas.org/content/101/46/16369.full>.

Government Office for Science (2008) *Mental Capital and Wellbeing: Making the Most of Ourselves in the 21st Century*, London.

Greene, J.D.; Sommerville, R.B.; Nystrom, L.E.; Darley, J.M.; and Cohen, J.D. (2001) 'An fMRI Investigation of Emotional Engagement in Moral Judgement', *Science*, 293(5537): 2105–2108.

Hamilton, D.R. (2010) *Why Kindness is Good for You*, Hay House.

House, J.S.; Lantz, P.M.; Herd, P. (2005) 'Continuity and Change in the Social Stratification of Aging and Health Over the Life Course: Evidence from a Nationally Representative Longitudinal Study from 1986 to 2001/2002', *The Journals of Gerontology Series B: Psychological Sciences and Social Sciences*, 60(SI2): 515–526.

Nitschke, J.B.; Nelson, E.E.; Rusch, B.D.; Fox, A.S.; Oakes, T.R.; and Davidson, R.J. (2004) 'Orbitofrontal Cortex Tracks Positive Mood in Mothers Viewing Pictures of their Newborn Infants', *NeuroImage*, 21(2): 583–592.

Pagano, M.E.; Friend, K.B.; Tonogan, J.S.; Stout, R.L. (2004) 'Helping Other Alcoholics in Alcoholics Anonymous and Drinks Outcome: Findings from Project Match', *Journal of Studies on Alcohol*, 65(6): 766–773.

Schwartz, C.E., and Sendor, M. (1999) 'Helping Others Helps Oneself: Response Shift Effects in Peer Support', *Social Science and Medicine*, 48(11): 1563–1575.

Thaddeus, W.W., *et al.* (2009) 'Effect of Compassion Meditation on Neuroendocrine Innate Immune and Behavioral Responses to Psychosocial Stress', *Psychoneuroendocrinology*, 34(1): 87–98.

5. PRACTISING GRATITUDE

Emmons, R.A., and McCullough, M.E. (2003) 'Counting Blessings versus Burdens: Experimental Studies of Gratitude and Subjective Well-Being', *Journal of Personality and Social Psychology*, 84(2): 377–389.

Emmons, R.A., and Crumpler, C.A. (2000) 'Gratitude as a Human Strength: Appraising the Evidence', *Journal of Social and Clinical Psychology*, 19(1): 56–69.

Emmons, R.A. (2007) 'Gratitude, Subjective Well-Being, and the Brain' in Eid, M., and Larsen, R.J. (eds), *The Science of Subjective Well-Being*, Guilford Press.

Emmons, R.A. (2008) *Thanks! How Practicing Gratitude Can Make You Happier*, Mariner.

Froh, J.J.; Sefick, W.J.; and Emmons, R.A. (2008) 'Counting Blessings in Early Adolescents: An Experimental Study of Gratitude and Subjective Wellbeing', *Journal of School Psychology*, 46(2): 213–233.

Gillham, J., and Reivich, K. (2004) 'Cultivating Optimism in Childhood and Adolescence', *The Annals of the American Academy of Political and Social Science*, 591(1): 146–163.

Gordon, A.M., *et al.* (2012) 'To Have and to Hold: Gratitude Promotes Relationship Maintenance in Intimate Bonds', *Journal of Personality and Social Psychology*, 103(2): 257–274.

Gottman, J.M., and Levenson, R.W. (1991) 'What Predicts Change in Marital Interaction Over Time? A Study of Alternative Models', *Family Processes Journal*, 38(2): 143–158.

Inoue, K. (2010) 'Cognitive Behavioral Therapy for Treatment Resistant-Depression', *Seishin Shinkeigaku Zasshi*, 112(11): 1097–1104.

Lambert, N.M.; Clark, M.S.; Durtschi, J.; Fincham, E.D.; and Graham, S.M. (2010) 'Benefits of Expressing Gratitude: Expressing Gratitude to a Partner Changes One's View of the Relationship', *Psychological Science*, 21(4): 574–580.

Lambert, N.M., and Fincham, F.D. (2011) 'Expressing Gratitude to a Partner Leads to More Relationship Maintenance Behaviour', *Emotion*, 11(1): 52–60.

Lyubomirsky, S. (2000) *The How of Happiness: A Practical Guide to Getting the Life You Want*, Piatkus Books.

Miller, T. (1995) *How to Want What You Have*, Harper Collins.

Nolen-Hoeksema, S. (2000) 'The Role of Rumination in Depressive Disorders and Mixed Anxiety/Depressive Symptoms', *Journal of Abnormal Psychology*, 109(3): 504–511.

Peterson, C., and Seligman, M. (2004) *Character Strengths and Virtues: A Classification and Handbook*, Oxford University Press.

Seligman, M.E.; Steen, T.A.; Park, N.; and Peterson, C. (2005) 'Positive Psychology Progress: Empirical Validation of Interventions', *American Psychologist*, 60(5): 410–421.

Wood, A.M.; Maltby, J.; Stewart, N.; and Stephen, J. (2008) 'Conceptualizing Gratitude and Appreciation as a Unitary Personality Trait', *Personality and Individual Differences*, 44(3): 621–632.

Wood, A.M.; Joseph, S.; Lloyd, J.; and Atkins, S. (2009) 'Gratitude Influences Sleep through the Mechanism of Pre-Sleep Cognitions', *Journal of Psychosomatic Research*, 66(1): 43–48.

6. SAVOURING

Bryant, F.B., and Veroff, J. (2006) *Savoring – A New Model of Positive Emotion*, Psychology Press.

Kabatznick, R. (1998) *The Zen of Eating – Ancient Answers to Modern Weight Problems*, TarcherPerigee.

Peterson, C. (2006) *A Primer in Positive Psychology*, Oxford University Press.

Quoidbach, J., *et al.* (2010) 'Money Giveth, Money Taketh Away: The Dual Effect of Wealth on Happiness', *Psychological Science*, 21(6): 759–763.

7. SPIRITUALITY AND PRAYER

Benson, H. (2000) 'Spirituality and Health: What We Know, What We Need to Know', *Journal of Social and Clinical Psychology*, 19(1): 102–116.

Casey, P. (2009) *The Psychosocial Benefits of Religious Practice*, Iona Institute.

Clark, A.E., and Lelkes, O. (2009) 'Let Us Pray: Religious Interactions in Life Satisfaction', *Paris School of Economics Working Papers*, n2009-01.

Dolan, P.; Peasgood, J.; and White, M. (2006) *Review of the Research on the Influences of Personal Wellbeing and Application to Public Policy Making*, Department for Environment, Food and Rural Affairs.

Duke University (1999) 'Religious Attendance Linked to Lower Mortality in Elderly', *ScienceDaily*: <www.sciencedaily.com/releases/1999/07/990726070153.htm

Ellison, C.G., and George, L.K. (1994) 'Religious Involvement, Social

References

Ties and Social Support in a Southeastern Community', *Journal for the Scientific Study of Religion*, 33(1): 46–61.

George, L.K.; Ellison, C.G.; and Larson, D.B. (2002) 'Explaining the Relationships between Religious Involvement and Health', *Psychological Inquiry*, 13(3): 190–200.

Harris, R.C., *et al.* (1995) 'The Role of Religion in Heart Transplant Recipients' Long-Term Health and Well-Being', *Journal of Religion and Health*, 34(1): 17–32.

Hummer, R.A.; Rogers, R.G.; Nam, C.B.; and Ellison, C.G. (1999) 'Religious Involvement and US Adult Mortality', *Demography*, 36(2): 273–285.

Koenig, H.G.; McCullough, M.; and Larson, D. (2001) *Handbook of Religious Health*, Oxford University Press.

Koenig, H.G., and Larson, D.B. (2001) 'Religion and Mental Health: Evidence for an Association', *International Review of Psychiatry*, 13(2): 67–78.

Levin, J.S., and Vanderpool, H.Y. (1987) 'Is Frequent Religious Attendance Really Conductive to Better Health? Towards an Epidemiology of Religion', *Social Science and Medicine*, 24(7): 589–600.

Levin, J.S., and Schiller, P.L. (1987) 'Is There a Religious Factor in Health?', *Journal of Religion in Health*, 26(1): 9–36.

McCullough, M.E.; Hoyt, W.J.; Larson, D.B.; Koenig, H.G.; and Thoresen, C. (2000) 'Religious Involvement and Mortality: A Meta-Analytic Review', *Health Psychology*, 19(3): 211–222.

Maltby, J.; Lewis, C.A.; and Day, L. (1999) 'Religious Orientation and Psychological Well-Being: The Role of the Frequency of Personal Prayer', *British Journal of Health Psychology*, 4(4): 363–378.

Miller, L., *et al.* (2014) 'Neuroanatomical Correlates of Religiosity and Spirituality: A Study in Adults at High and Low Familial Risk for Depression', *JAMA Psychiatry*, 71(2): 128–135.

Powell, L., *et al.* (2003) 'Religion and Spirituality: Linkages to Physical Health', *American Psychologist*, 58(1): 36–52.

Oxman, T.E.; Freeman, D.H.; and Manheimer, E.D. (1995) 'Lack of Social Participation or Religious Strength and Comfort as Risk Factors for Death after Cardiac Surgery in the Elderly', *Psychosomatic Medicine*, 57(1): 5–15.

Spiegel, D.; Bloom, J.R.; Kraemer, H.C.; and Gottheil, E. (1989) 'Effect of Psychosocial Treatment of Patients with Metastatic Breast Cancer', *Lancet*, 2: 888–891.

Wallace, J.M., and Forman, T.A. (1998) 'Religion's Role in Promoting Health and Reducing Risk Among American Youth', *Health Education and Behaviour*, 25(6): 721–741.

Walsh, K., *et al.* (2002) 'Spiritual Beliefs May Affect Outcome of Bereavement: A Prospective Study', *British Medical Journal*, 324(7353): 1551–1556.

8. BOUNCIBILITY

Durlak, J.A. (1998) 'Common Risk Factors in Successful Prevention Programs', *American Journal of Orthopsychiatry*, 68(4): 512–520.

Hiroto, D.S., and Seligman, M.E. (1975) 'Generality of Learned Helplessness in Man', *Journal of Personality and Social Psychology*, 31(2): 311–327.

Maier, S.F., and Seligman, M.E. (1976) 'Learned Helplessness: Theory and Evidence', *Journal of Experimental Psychology General*, 105(1): 3–46.

Masten, A.S. (2001) 'Ordinary Magic: Resilience Processes in Development', *American Psychologist*, 56(3): 227–238.

Reivich, K., and Shatte, A. (2002) *The Resilience Factor: 7 Essential Skills for Overcoming Life's Inevitable Obstacles*, Broadway Books.

Seligman, M.E. (1990) *Learned Optimism: How to Change Your Mind and Your Life,* Vintage Books.

9. PEOPLE NEED PEOPLE

Berkman, L.F., and Syme, S.L. (1979) 'Social Networks, Host Resistance and Mortality: A Nine Year Follow Study of Alameda County Residents', *American Journal of Epidemiology*, 109(2): 186–204.

Cacioppo, J., and Hawley, L.C. (2005) 'Loneliness and Pathways to Disease', *Brain, Behaviour and Immunity*, 17(1): 98–105.

Holt-Lunstad, J.; Smith, T.B.; and Layton, J.B. (2010) 'Social Relationships and Mortality Risk: A Meta-Analytic Review', *PLoS Medicine*, 7(7): e1000316.

House, J.S.; Robbins, C.; and Metzner, H.L. (1982) 'The Association of Social Relationships and Activities with Mortality: Prospective Evidence from the Tecumseh Community Health Study', *America Journal of Epidemiology*, 116(11): 123–140.

Kraut, R., *et al.* (1998) 'Internet Paradox: A Social Technology that Reduces Social Involvement and Psychological Well Being', *American Psychologist*, 53(9): 1017–1031.

McPherson, M., *et al.* (2006) 'Discussion Networks over Two Decades', *American Sociological Review*, 71(3): 353–375.

Ruston, D. (2003) *Volunteers, Helpers and Socialisers: Social Capital and Time Use*, Office for National Statistics, London.

Sigman, A. (2007) 'Visual Voodoo: The Biological Impact of Watching Television', *Biologist*, 54(1): 14–19.

10. MIND YOUR BODY

Craft, L.L., and Perna, F.M. (2004) 'The Benefits of Exercise for the Clinically Depressed', *Primary Care Companion to the Journal of Clinical Psychiatry*, 6(3): 104–111.

Wang, Y., and Lobstein, T. (2006) 'Worldwise Trends in Childhood Over-weight and Obesity', *International Journal of Pediatric Obesity*, 1(1): 11–25.

Williams, J., *et al.* (2009) *Growing Up in Ireland: National Longitudinal Study of Children*, The Stationery Office, 58.

11. AM I HERE AT ALL? INTRODUCING MINDFULNESS INTO YOUR WORLD

Chambers, R.; Chuen Yee Lo, B.; and Allen, N.B. (2008) 'The Impact of Intensive Mindfulness Training on Attentional Control, Cognitive Style, and Affect', *Cognitive Therapy and Research*, 32(3): 303–322.

Davidson, R.J., *et al.* (2003) 'Alterations in Brain and Immune Function Produced by Mindfulness Meditation', *Psychosomatic Medicine*, 65(4): 564–570.

Grossman, P., *et al.* (2004) 'Mindfulness-Based Stress Reduction and Health Benefits: A Meta-Analysis', *Journal of Psychosomatic Research*, 57(1): 35–43.

Jha, A.P.; Krompinger, J.; and Baime, M.J. (2007) 'Mindfulness Training Modifies Subsystems of Attention', *Cognitive, Affective and Behavioural Neuroscience*, 7(2): 109–119.

Lazar, S.W., *et al.* (2005) 'Meditation Experience Is Associated with Increased Cortical Thickness', *Neuroreport*, 16(17): 1893–1897.

Leach, A. (2015) 'One of San Francisco's Toughest Schools Transformed by the Power of Meditation', *The Guardian* (London), 24 November.

Marchand, W.R. (2012) 'Mindfulness-Based Stress Reduction, Mindfulness-Based Cognitive Therapy and Zen Meditation for Depression, Anxiety Pain and Psychological Distress', *Journal of Psychiatric Practice*, 18(4): 233–252.

Rinske, A., *et al.* (2015) 'Standardised Mindfulness-Based Interventions in Healthcare: An Overview of Systematic Reviews and Meta-Analyses of RCTs', *PLoS ONE*, 10(4): e0124344.

Tang, Y., *et al.* (2007) 'Short-Term Meditation Training Improves Attention and Self-Regulation', *Proceedings of the National Academy of Sciences of the USA*, 104(43): 17152–17156.

Weare, K. (2012) *Evidence for the Impact of Mindfulness on Children and Young People*: available on <https://mindfulnessinschools.org/wp-content/uploads/2013/02/MiSP-Research-Summary-2012.pdf>.

Zeidan, F.; Johnston, S.K.; Diamond, B.J.; David, Z.; and Goolkasian, P. (2010) 'Mindfulness Meditation Improves Cognition: Evidence of Brief Mental Training', *Conscious Cognition*, 19(2): 597–605.